THE IDEA OF IMMORTALITY

Oxford University Press

London Edinburgh Glasgow Copenhagen
New York Toronto Melbourne Cape Town
Bombay Calcutta Madras Shanghai

Humphrey Milford Publisher to the UNIVERSITY

THE IDEA OF IMMORTALITY

The Gifford Lectures

DELIVERED IN THE UNIVERSITY OF EDINBURGH
IN THE YEAR 1922

BY

A. SETH PRINGLE-PATTISON
LL.D., D.C.L.
FELLOW OF THE BRITISH ACADEMY
EMERITUS PROFESSOR OF LOGIC AND METAPHYSICS IN THE
UNIVERSITY OF EDINBURGH

OXFORD
AT THE CLARENDON PRESS
1922

2562

Printed in England

TO

THE EARL OF BALFOUR, K.G., O.M.

IN GRATEFUL REMEMBRANCE

OF THE OPPORTUNITY PROVIDED

BY HIS FOUNDATION OF

THE BALFOUR PHILOSOPHICAL LECTURESHIP

NOW FORTY YEARS AGO

AND OF THE LONG FRIENDSHIP THUS BEGUN

PREFACE

THESE Lectures may be regarded as in some sense a sequel to those delivered on the Gifford Foundation in the University of Aberdeen and afterwards published as *The Idea of God.* The question with which they deal was touched upon there incidentally at several points, but more by way of implication than of direct argument. Perhaps these indications might have been taken as sufficient; for a writer's conclusions on such a subject are the natural outcome of his general philosophical position, and specific argument about immortality has not been notably successful or profitable in the past. But the place and destiny of the finite individual became the subject of an animated discussion, starting from certain statements in *The Idea of God*, in a Symposium of the Aristotelian Society held in the summer of 1918. And when Principal Jacks conveyed to me in 1920 an invitation from the Hibbert Trustees to deliver a short course of lectures in Oxford, and intimated at the same time a strong desire that I should take Immortality as my subject, it seemed almost incumbent upon me to endeavour to meet the wish thus expressed. The six lectures delivered in Manchester College in the Lent Term of 1921 have been refashioned and elaborated, with considerable additions, to form the present course. I have to thank the Hibbert Trustees for their courtesy in leaving me perfectly free to use the material of my Oxford lectures for this further purpose. It would have been impossible for me otherwise to accept their invitation, and the pleasure of lecturing in Oxford and of meeting students and teachers there is one which I would not willingly have missed.

To my former colleagues in the University of Edinburgh, who so unexpectedly appointed me Gifford Lecturer in my old University, I can but tender my grateful thanks for the spirit which prompted their action. As I had already held the corresponding Lectureship in the University of Aberdeen, the offer took me completely by surprise. I considered that I had already enjoyed the opportunity which such a position confers. But the generous confidence which the invitation implied made it difficult, if not impossible, to refuse, and was in itself an incitement to further study and reflection.

The present volume represents the first series of lectures, delivered during the academic year 1921–2. It does not claim for a moment to exhaust a subject to which the avenues of approach are so many and so varied; but the survey taken and the line of argument followed reach in the course of these ten lectures their natural conclusion. Hence it has seemed to me most appropriate to publish this series by itself, without waiting for the second, still to be delivered, in which I hope to discuss some other fundamental religious ideas.

In preparing the lectures for the press I have been much indebted to my brother, Professor James Seth, to Mr. H. F. Hallett, my former Assistant, now Lecturer in the University of Leeds, and, not least, to Mr. J. B. Capper, my oldest friend. I take this opportunity of thanking them for the care they have bestowed upon the proofs and for many valuable suggestions which have often enabled me to clarify the argument and to improve its form.

Edinburgh, *October* 1922.

CONTENTS

LECTURE I

PRIMITIVE IDEAS OF THE SOUL AND THE AFTER-LIFE

PAGE

The universality of the belief in some future life 1
The argument from universality not conclusive 2
The crudeness of its early expressions does not prove a belief to be false 4
Primitive idea of death as an unnatural intrusion 5
Body and soul in animistic philosophy 7
Ideas of the spirit-land 10
Theories of continuance *v.* theories of retribution 13
Development of the belief dependent on its ethical and religious significance 14

LECTURE II

THE HEBREWS AND THE GREEKS: A PARALLEL DEVELOPMENT

Non-ethical character of the Hebrew Sheol 15
The individual and the nation 17
Belief in personal immortality late in appearance and based on experience of communion with God 18
The Homeric Hades 20
The sepulchral reliefs and inscriptions of classical Greece . . 22
The cult of Dionysus and the mystical identification of the worshipper with the god 23
Orphic doctrine of the origin and destiny of the soul . . . 25
Orphic influence on later religious thought and practice . . 28

LECTURE III

PRE-EXISTENCE AND IMMORTALITY IN PLATO

The primacy of the soul throughout the Platonic Dialogues . 33
Its pre-existence and heavenly origin 35
The world of Ideas or Forms 38
The 'eternal' or 'divine' life of reason 39

PAGE

How much of the soul survives the death of the body? . . . 41
Specific arguments for immortality 44
'All knowledge is recollection' 46
The argument though philosophically valuable fails to prove individual pre-existence 48
Function of the Myth in Plato's teaching 51
The disinterestedness and self-sufficingness of virtue 54
Practical character of religious truth 57
The mystic and ascetic element in the *Phaedo* 59
Serenity of Plato's general outlook 60

LECTURE IV

MIND AND BODY

The contrast between Plato and Aristotle 62
Aristotle's start from the biological facts 63
The soul as the 'entelechy' or 'fulfilment' of the body . . 65
The distinction between the 'Active' and the 'Passive' Reason 66
The Scholastic doctrine of 'the rational soul' 69
The soul as an immaterial or spiritual substance 72
Its unity and simplicity the guarantee of its immortality . . 73
The futility of such soul-substances in the explanation of our conscious life 75
Lotze's critical revision of the traditional conception of substance 77
The soul conceived as a unitary being in which physical movements by their impact produce effects 82

LECTURE V

MIND AND BODY (*continued*)

Resultant theories of the relation of mind and body: (1) Crude Materialism 83
(2) Epiphenomenalism or conscious automatism 84
(3) Psycho-physical Parallelism 86
The underlying presupposition of all such theories is their conception of the body as a pure machine 88
The living body as the embodied soul 91
The organism an analogue of the kind of unity characteristic of the self-conscious being 92
False ideal of the unchanging unit 93
Hume's criticism of such a self unanswerable 96
William James's view of the passing thought as the only thinker 98

PAGE

The systematic unity of the mind 99
All conscious experience presupposes an individual subject . 101
Resultant conception of the spiritual self 104

LECTURE VI

REINCARNATION AND KARMA

Transmigration in primitive thought 106
The doctrine of Karma as a vindication of cosmic justice . . 109
Illusory character of the identity between the successive individuals 113
The theory not based on the real facts of moral causation . . 117
An ethical postulate, not a scientific law 118
Misconceptions of the real nature of the theory 121
Dr. McTaggart's 'metaphysical argument' for pre-existence and immortality 123
The assumption of a fixed number of souls 127

LECTURE VII

ETERNAL LIFE

Conflict of human sentiment with regard to a future life . . 131
Horror of the endless progress 133
Eternal life as a present experience 135
Modes of its realization: intellectual, aesthetic, and religious . 136
Eternal life in New Testament usage 139
Jesus and St. Paul 141
The Fourth Gospel and the Johannine Epistles 144
The Buddhist Nirvana 145

LECTURE VIII

ETERNAL LIFE AND PERSONAL IMMORTALITY

Is 'eternal life' in the present offered in place of a further life after death? 148
History of Spinoza's views on immortality 149
Professor Bosanquet's attitude: 'moralism *v.* religion' . . 153
The significance of spiritual growth 155
Absolutism and the individual 156
Absorption in the object: the higher and the lower mysticism . 159
The idea of reabsorption based on physical analogies . . . 162
Some believers in a future life still contemplate reabsorption as a final consummation 164

LECTURE IX

SOME ARGUMENTS REVIEWED

PAGE

The meaning of the 'substantiality' of the soul again considered 168
Butler's argument from the moral government of the world . 171
Retributive punishment 173
Kant and Sidgwick on the correlation of virtue and happiness . 176
The discrepancy between individual and social good 178
Is belief in immortality an indispensable condition of moral conduct and of religious faith? 181
Tennyson and Epictetus contrasted 184
The Stoic and the Christian mood 186

LECTURE X

CONCLUSIONS

The fundamental argument is from the divine perfection . . 190
The argument from desire insecure so long as desire remains selfish 192
The objectivity of our ideals 193
Immortality neither a natural possession nor a talismanic gift . 195
'Those who in their lifetime were never alive' 197
Hume's negative conclusion depends on his arbitrary restriction of the meaning of 'reason' 198
The idea of universal restoration 202
Two contrasted attitudes towards death and the after-life . . 206

LECTURE I

PRIMITIVE IDEAS OF THE SOUL AND THE AFTER-LIFE.

THE universality of a belief is no sufficient guarantee of its truth. Yet there is undeniably something very impressive in the unanimity with which man, from the first dim beginnings of his planetary history, has refused to see in death the end of his being and activities. 'The grassy barrows' scattered over our moors and uplands bear eloquent, if pathetic and often gruesome, testimony to the undoubting faith of those who laid their dead there. In a still remoter past, the cave-men of the Palaeolithic age, more than 20,000 years ago, laid their dead reverently to rest with the same belief in a further life. Explorations in France, in the caves of the Dordogne, within the last twenty years, have brought to light a number of instances of such ceremonial interment, exhibiting the excavated grave, the carefully disposed skeleton with offerings of food and implements laid beside the body for use in the life beyond.[1]

It was the same ancient hunters, of a somewhat later period, who have left us on the walls or roofs of their cave-dwellings, or carved on the bone and ivory of their implements, studies of animals singly or in groups, so convincing in their reality and so masterly in their technique, that critics entitled to judge have declared these paintings in the caves of France and Spain to be superior in artistic sense and execution to all but the best modern pictures of similar subjects. Thus, from the

[1] Sollas, *Ancient Hunters*, p. 181.

beginning, in these two ways—by the perception of beauty evinced in his artistic mastery of line and colour on the one hand, and, on the other, by his outlook beyond this visible scene—man, that strange animal, seems to be lifted above his kindred in ways which it is easier to appreciate than to explain. His life is in another dimension than theirs. The sense of immortality, Wordsworth remarks in his 'Essay on Epitaphs', if not a co-existent and twin-birth with Reason, is among the earliest of her offspring. And indeed the very custom of reverent burial, unknown to any other species, and the feelings which prompt us 'to look upon the dust of man with awe'[1] may quite properly be regarded as an index of the endowment which, despite man's animal ancestry and his gradual emergence from a brutish state, puts, in Locke's words, 'a perfect distinction betwixt man and brutes',[2] and makes him an historical being and a creature capable of religion.

Nevertheless, as I said at the outset, the universality of a belief cannot be regarded as a sufficient guarantee of its truth, and the argument from the *consensus gentium* has always suffered from the difficulty of defining in what the *consensus* consists. Hence, when the argument is put forward in support of the existence of God—perhaps its most common application—we find ourselves confronted by recurring debates between eminent authorities as to the existence or non-existence of 'tribes of atheists', races, that is to say, entirely without the conception of God and destitute of any properly religious ideas. Travellers and missionaries report in a positive or negative sense according to the preconceived ideas they attach to the terms. It is easy enough to establish the absence of religious ideas, if we identify religion with a clear Theistic belief in the moral government of the world, or

[1] Wordsworth, *Excursion*, Bk. V. [2] *Essay*, Bk. II. 11. 10.

draw some arbitrary distinction between 'superstition' and 'religion'. The immense extension of anthropological research within the last half-century, introducing us, as never before, into the workings of the primitive mind, has at least put an end to such profitless disputes. But, on the other hand, the complicated irrationality and absurdity of the beliefs which it reveals as the basis of the earliest rites and practices which can be termed religious, easily suggest the conclusion that whatever springs from such a root must be infected with similar delusions and can bear little relation to the nature of things. However religion may be transformed in the course of its history, the circumstances of its origin and the nature of its earliest associations and accompaniments seem to many minds to make it incurably suspect. Yet Sir James Frazer, who, more perhaps than any other man, has flooded us with records of the irrationalities and immoralities of primitive cults and beliefs, can write thus in the Preface to *Psyche's Task*: 'Man is a very curious animal, and the more we know of his habits, the more curious does he appear. He may be the most rational of the beasts, but certainly he is the most absurd. . . . Yet the odd thing is that in spite of, and perhaps in virtue of, his absurdities man moves steadily upwards. . . . From false premises he often arrives at sound conclusions; from a chimerical theory he deduces a salutary practice.' The book in question, he says, is intended to illustrate 'a few of the ways in which folly mysteriously deviates into wisdom, and good comes out of evil. If the colours are dark they are yet illuminated by a ray of consolation and hope.' Such a passage is, in effect, an acknowledgement, in a quarter from which one might hardly have expected it, of what philosophers have called the unconscious reason operative in human history, guiding men to issues beyond the scope of their immediate purpose or the compass of their conscious reflection. It is the salutary warning, *Respice finem*, await the issue. It is a radical fallacy in philosophical method to seek to 'explain' any phenomenon, and to rob it of its significance, by identifying it with its first crude beginning, the first gross and fantastic ceremonies in which historical research can detect its presence. It is only in the light of what it grows to, that we can interpret the germ. Historical beginnings are interesting or important only in virtue of their continuity with the later and more adequate expressions of the principle which they dimly exemplify.

This warning is very necessary in connexion with the belief in immortality. 'Among savage races', says Sir James Frazer, 'a life after death is not a matter of speculation and conjecture, of hope and fear; it is a practical certainty which the individual as little dreams of doubting as he doubts the reality of his conscious existence. He assumes it without inquiry and acts upon it without hesitation, as if it were one of the best ascertained truths within the limits of human experience.'[1] But few would now endorse Lessing's view that 'the first and oldest opinion is, in matters of speculation, always the most probable, because common sense immediately hit upon it'.[2] Rather do the primitive illusions and superstitions in which the idea of the soul and its separate existence first took shape seem to many minds to invalidate all later forms of the same idea. No conclusion, however, could be more fallacious. The roots of a belief may be deeper than the associations which suggested it or the flimsy arguments at first advanced in its support. These are soon discarded or forgotten, but the progress of thought consists in penetrating to the true

[1] *Belief in Immortality*, p. 468.

[2] Note to the tract, *Dass mehr als fünf Sinne für den Menschen sein können.*

grounds on which the belief rests, and, in the process, recasting the belief itself.

What, then, is the actual nature of the primitive belief in an after-life which we find so universally diffused? Its main features have been made familiar to us by the anthropologists. Many savage tribes, it has been shown, not only believe in a life after death: they believe in the natural immortality of man in his present state of existence. The unconscious logic of their belief appears to be that whatever lives will go on living indefinitely, unless brought to a violent end by the blow of an enemy or the even more dangerous arts of the sorcerer. Knowing nothing of the physical conditions of life—the organic cycle of growth and decay which links birth and death together as equally natural incidents in a single process—they look upon death as a wholly unnatural intrusion. They have not framed the conception of what we call a 'natural' death. At the lowest stage they do not even recognize disease as a cause of death, or at least they treat it, not as a natural visitation, but as due to witchcraft. For them every death is therefore a violent death, an interference with the course of nature. 'No great man', says an observer of the Melanesian natives, 'would like to be told that he was ill by natural weakness or decay':[1] it would be an affront to his dignity.

It is consonant with this view of natural or inherent immortality that, at a certain stage of culture, we find a variety of myths current to explain the origin of death—that is to say, how death got a footing in the world at all. Some of these stories connect themselves with the phenomenon of the waxing and the waning moon. In the happier 'long ago', it is sometimes said, death was unknown or rather it was a short sleep. Men died on the last day of the waning moon and came to life again three

[1] Quoted by Frazer, *op. cit.*, p. 55.

days after, on the first appearance of the new moon, as if they had awakened from a refreshing slumber. But an evil spirit somehow contrived that when men slept the sleep of death they should wake no more. Another type of story is based on the biological fact that certain animals, such as serpents and lizards, periodically shed their skins, and appear therefore to the savage observer to enjoy a natural immortality. If man could only cast his old skin once a year—the reasoning proceeds—he too would renew his life perennially like the serpent. And this was the destiny originally intended for the human race by a beneficent creator. It was his will that man should live, and that the serpents, whom he hated, should die. But his message conveying the secret of immortality was perverted by the stupidity or malice of the messenger to whom it was entrusted; and that is why all creatures are now subject to death, except the serpent, who, when he is old, casts his skin and so lives for ever. The feather-brained messenger who turns the message upside down, or the messenger who lingers to refresh himself by the way, and so allows himself to be forestalled by his fellow who delivers the message in a precisely contrary sense, is a frequent figure in these stories.[1] For another type of such explanatory tales we need not go farther than the Hebrew story

> Of man's first disobedience, and the fruit
> Of that forbidden tree whose mortal taste
> Brought death into the world, and all our woe.

But, to whatever cause the liability to die may be attributed, the fact of death inevitably comes to be regarded as part of the ordinance of nature. The primitive belief in the persistence of life is not affected, however, by this acquiescence. This is rendered possible by the

[1] Cf. Frazer, *op. cit.*, Lecture III, Myths of the Origin of Death.

'animism' which is a prevailing characteristic of primitive thought. Although he is far from being able to conceive an immaterial or purely spiritual being, primitive man is still farther from being a materialist in the philosophical meaning of the term—in the sense, namely, of explaining everything that happens as the result of purely physical causes and laws. On the contrary, the distinction between body and soul is the first product of his reflection and forms the starting-point of all his explanations of natural phenomena. To us, with our modern scientific ideas, it seems supremely irrational to attribute natural events to the personal agency of a swarming multitude of spirits or ghosts; but for the savage such a theory is really an effort to rationalize, to give a causal explanation of the pell-mell of occurrences which constitutes his daily experience. It is the earliest system of natural philosophy. And there is nothing surprising in the fact that man took his first idea of cause from the only form of agency with which he was directly acquainted, his own acts of will. Familiar sequences do not ordinarily arouse attention: they do not seem to call for explanation. To that extent something like the reign of law in the modern scientific sense is no doubt tacitly presupposed, within certain limits, even in the most rudimentary savage conception of the world and the course of events. But everything out of the way that happens to him, 'every stumble over a stone,' as Tylor says, 'every odd sound or feeling, every time he loses his way in the woods', is attributed to the agency of friendly, or more frequently unfriendly, spirits.[1]

The notion of soul or ghost or spirit was thus first framed by primitive man as an explanation of certain features of his experience; and there is no reason to

[1] *Anthropology*, p. 356. Cf. D'Alviella's article on Animism in Hastings's *Encyclopaedia of Religion and Ethics*.

question the importance attached by anthropologists to the phenomena of sleep and dreams in this connexion. In sleep the body lies like a log without sense or motion; the principle of life and movement appears to be absent. On awaking, the man recalls the dreams he has had in the interval; he has travelled great distances and met people known to him whom he has not seen for many a day, friends who have gone to some other district or who perhaps are dead. As the body has remained all the time motionless in the same place—a fact to which others can testify—his natural conclusion is that these expeditions have been undertaken by a second self or double, which can leave the body and return to it again. All men and animals have such doubles or souls, which behave in the same way; and when figures appear to him in dreams in his own home-surroundings, our primitive dreamer concludes that the souls of distant or dead friends have actually come to visit him while he slept. And inasmuch as the figures seen in dreams, whether of the living or of the dead, appear in the garb and accoutrements familiar to our waking experience, the savage unhesitatingly endows even inanimate things with similar phantasmal souls. So, in *Hamlet*, 'the majesty of buried Denmark' wears 'the very armour he had on, when he the ambitious Norway combated'. To primitive philosophy the armour possesses the same kind of reality as the ghost it encloses. And this accords with the burial customs of savages and barbarians. The garments and ornaments, the weapons and implements, that are laid in the tomb or burnt upon the funeral pyre are not *themselves* supposed to be carried by the dead into the life beyond. Their bodies are buried or burnt like his; it is their shadow-souls which the phantom wears or wields in the spirit-land.[1] The savage

[1] The fact that the buried implements have often been deliberately broken points to the same conclusion.

philosophy is on this point quite consistent. The same thing applies to the food provided for the dead: it is not actually but spiritually partaken of. A Jesuit Father, writing in the seventeenth century, tells us that the missionaries in Cochin China, who tried to convince the natives of the irrationality of their practice of providing sumptuous banquets several times a year for the dead, were met by ridicule of their ignorance. Translating the philosophical distinctions of the natives into his own scholastic terminology, the Father concludes hopefully that 'it may be judged from the distinctions they make between the accidents and the substance of the food they prepare for the dead, that it will not be very difficult to prove to them the mystery of the Eucharist'.[1]

The primitive idea of the soul makes it thus 'an ethereal image of the body'.[2] The resemblance is supposed to be complete, wounds and mutilations of the body being reproduced in its shadowy counterpart. 'The Australian who has slain his enemy will cut off the right thumb of the corpse, so that, although the spirit will become a hostile ghost, it cannot throw with its mutilated hand the shadowy spear, and may be safely left to wander, malignant but harmless.'[3] The soul is ethereal, tenuous or filmy in consistence, and possesses the power of flashing quickly from place to place; but many customs, such as that of leaving apertures for it to pass through, or of spreading ashes to track the footsteps of a ghostly visitor, prove that it was not conceived as purely immaterial.

Such, then, is the primitive idea of the soul which, in the case of man, is believed to survive bodily death, carrying with it the consciousness and volition of the dead man, and able to visit its pleasure or displeasure upon survivors by producing effects in the physical world. The last point is important, for it was on account of their supposed

[1] Tylor, *Primitive Culture*, ii. 41. [2] *Ibid.*, i. 450. [3] *Ibid.*, i. 451.

power to benefit or to hurt the living that the cult or tendance of the dead became such a prominent feature in primitive societies. Fear and love mingle at first as motives in these rites; for ghosts are a capricious folk, and one never knows at what they may take offence. As one observer of the savage mind put it, 'There is a certain malignity in the feeling of all ghosts towards the living, who offend them by being alive.'[1] Hence the uneasiness of the living, and the elaborate precautions frequently taken to prevent the ghost of the dead man from finding his way back to the house which he occupied in life. But the more prevalent attitude, especially as we pass to more advanced stages of culture, is that naturally suggested by family affection or clan-feeling; and the character of these funeral and memorial observances takes on an aspect more uniformly benign. Offerings and ceremonies which may have been prompted at first, in part at least, by a desire to propitiate or placate, are continued as disinterested tokens of remembrance and affection.

As to the nature of the after-life, and its locality, we can hardly expect to be able to reduce savage beliefs to a coherent system. There is a general belief, persisting to a late date, that in the interval between death and burial the spirit continues to hover in the neighbourhood of the body; and the unburied dead are supposed to be condemned to wander for ever, aimless and miserable, upon the face of the earth. But some rites seem to imply the belief that, even after the burial of the body, the soul either inhabits the grave (or the little soul-hut erected upon it), or lingers, at all events, in its vicinity. This appears to be the original meaning of the offerings of food and drink placed upon the tomb, especially when we read of shafts or pipes being sunk into the ground by which

[1] Quoted by Frazer, *op. cit.*, p. 55.

these refreshments may be conveyed to 'the poor inhabitant below'. The aborigines of Australia, again, 'imagine that the spirits of the dead continue to haunt their native land, and especially certain striking natural features of the landscape: it may be a pool of water in a deep gorge of the barren hills, or a solitary tree in the sun-baked plains, or a great rock that affords a welcome shade in the sultry noon. Such spots are thought to be tenanted by the souls of the departed. There they lurk, constantly on the watch for passing women, into whom they may enter, and from whom, in due time, they may be born as infants.'[1] But such crude imaginings are hardly representative. The dead who have received the rites of sepulture are usually conceived as setting out on a journey to some distant land of spirits, situated, it may be, in the traditional home-land from which the ancestors of their race have trekked, or figured at other times as some earthly paradise in the west. Sometimes this spirit-land is located in the skies, but oftenest, perhaps, as suggested by earth-burial, in some more sombre region under the earth. It is apparently to meet the perils and fatigues of this journey that some of the objects placed beside the dead in the tomb are provided. Life in the spirit-land is a ghostly continuation of the life led here. Death brings with it no change of character, no widening of outlook or deepening of feeling. The dead are thought of as pursuing their old activities and interests, or ruminating upon the 'good hunting' of their earthly days. The familiar tribal environment, with its sharply marked distinctions of social rank, is projected into the life beyond; a chief here is a chief there, and has a fitting retinue to support his dignity. In some more aristocratically minded tribes, indeed, it is only the chief and the higher orders who

[1] *Ibid.*, p. 83.

survive: 'the lower ranks were believed to be endowed with souls that died with their bodies'.[1]

This primitive belief in a further life is not, of course, a belief in immortality in the strict or philosophical sense of an endless life. Such a conception of endlessness we may well consider to be beyond the grasp of primitive man: it is too abstract. He is not accustomed to carry his thoughts backward beyond the generations he has himself known or been told of, and his thoughts of the future have an equally narrow horizon. 'Ask the negro', says one explorer, 'where is the spirit of his great-grandfather; he says he does not know, it is done. Ask him about the spirits of his father or brother who died yesterday, then he is full of fear and terror.'[2] This is crudely put, yet it is but the counterpart of Maeterlinck's touching fancy,[3] according to which the land of the dead is indeed 'the land of memory', the inhabitants of which awake to life and consciousness only when the thoughts of the living turn towards them in love. Obviously such personal memories cannot extend beyond two or three generations, and accordingly there is no vivid sense of the continued existence of the countless generations of the past. This ebbing of the soul's vitality with the lapse of time is expressed naïvely in some of these primitive eschatologies. The Mexicans held, for example, that while warriors and some others, after four years in paradise, become birds of beautiful plumage in the celestial gardens, the common lot was to pass to the underworld of Mictlan in the far north, 'a most obscure land where light cometh not and whence none can ever return'. Mictlan had nine divisions,

[1] Tylor, *Primitive Culture*, ii. 22. So, in Uganda, the bodies of the common people used to be cast out unburied, while those of the chiefs were mummified in a rude way and interred. Cf. Salmond, *Christian Doctrine of Immortality*, p. 17.

[2] Du Chaillu, quoted by Spencer, *Principles of Sociology*, i. 198.

[3] In *The Blue Bird*.

through which the progress of the spirits necessarily led them, and at the end of the fourth year they reached the ninth and ceased to be. Similarly, common souls in passing from one division to another of the Maori Hades, lost a little of their vitality each time, till at last they died outright.[1] Usually of course no such positive limits are laid down, and the continuance appears to be indefinite; but the question has not been thought out, can hardly be said to have been raised.

A more important point in connexion with these early beliefs is that they are not inspired by any ethical or religious motives. The future life, at this stage, is often, no doubt, painted as a 'better world', in so far as it is an idealization of present conditions. 'The American Indian's paradise will be full of game; the land of the Greenlander's hope is one of perpetual summer and no night, good water and superfluity of birds and fish, seals and reindeer, to be caught without difficulty or found alive seething in a great kettle; the Norseman's Walhalla gives him his fill of fighting and of feasting'.[2] But these pictures concern only the material conditions of existence; they do not represent the future state of existence as in any sense a 'higher' life, a 'fulfilment', so to say, of the present life, a realization of what we have imperfectly striven after here. Nor is it thought of as a 'dread assize', a scheme of rewards and punishments for deeds done in the body. The lot of the dead is not determined at all by what we ordinarily call moral considerations; they simply live on there as here. Hence Tylor, following Captain Burton, distinguishes theories of this type as 'theories of continuance' from what these writers call 'retribution theories' of the future life.[3]

[1] J. Estlin Carpenter, *Comparative Religion*, pp. 232–4.
[2] Tylor, *op. cit.*, ii. 77.
[3] Still one must not make such a distinction too rigid. When courage,

Retribution is a word of evil omen, and the conception of the future life as essentially a system of rewards and punishments is, I believe, a hopelessly inadequate and even distorted idea of it. But, however the notion of retribution or compensation may have been abused, it is plain enough that theories which involve it spring from a deeper experience than theories of mere continuance, in which the question of the moral order of the world has not yet been raised. It would be easy, in fact, to show from history that only so far as popular ideas of the future life take on an ethical or religious colouring does the belief acquire significance for a tribe or nation, or show any capacity of development into a higher doctrine. The idea of mere continuance in itself leads nowhere, just because it has no moral or religious value.

This is strikingly exemplified in the popular beliefs both of the Greeks and of the Hebrews—and, it may be added, of the Romans. To these three nations we owe nearly all the elements of our European civilization; yet in none of them, during the longest and most brilliant period of their history, did popular or traditional belief about the soul advance beyond the stage of primitive animism. This instance of arrested development is so remarkable, and its consequences are so instructive for the further progress of our argument, that, although I feel I am traversing well-known ground, I will venture in the next lecture to recall briefly some of the relevant facts.

endurance, skill, and enterprise are represented as affecting a man's place and destiny in the other world, we have already the recognition of moral distinctions in the future life, although the morality recognized may be of a primitive and rudimentary type, as was naturally to be expected.

LECTURE II

THE HEBREWS AND THE GREEKS: A PARALLEL DEVELOPMENT

In the case of the Hebrews we very commonly hear it said that during the whole of their history as an independent nation they possessed no doctrine of individual immortality, and the statement, as we shall see, is substantially true. Its substantial truth is, in fact, just what I wish to emphasize. But it must not be taken to mean that there did not exist among them a generally accepted belief in the survival of the soul. They combined with the worship of Jahveh an eschatology of a genuinely primitive type, described by Archdeacon Charles as 'a piece of true Semitic heathenism'.[1] Sheol was the name they gave to the gloomy abode of the dead in the lowest parts of the earth, and it is frequently described as 'the pit' into which the dead go down. It is 'a land of darkness', we read in the Book of Job, 'as darkness itself, and of the shadow of death, without any order, and where the light is as darkness'.[2] This is 'the house appointed for all living',[3] the final abode alike of the righteous and the wicked. Such distinctions have indeed no meaning in the underworld, for it is completely beyond the jurisdiction of Jahveh. Jahveh was worshipped as a god of justice and righteousness, but originally and pre-eminently as the national god; and, as such, his dominion and his worship were confined, as in the case of other tribal gods, strictly within his own territorial limits. So it was with the gods of the surrounding nations, Chemosh the god of the Moabites, Milcom

[1] *Doctrine of a Future Life* (2nd ed.), p. 3. [2] Job x. 22. [3] xxx. 23.

the god of the Ammonites, Ashtoreth of the Zidonians, and many more. David complains to Saul, accordingly, that he has been driven forth from his own country and forced thereby to forsake the worship of Jahveh for the service of other gods.[1] If Jahveh is thus not even the God of the whole earth, still less does his jurisdiction extend to Sheol. In one of the Psalms the writer speaks of 'the slain that lie in the grave, whom thou rememberest no more, and they are cut off from thy hand'.[2] It is no more than literal truth, therefore, to say that relations between Jahveh and his worshipper were supposed to cease entirely at death. The contrast between the living and the dead is vividly brought home to us in the thanksgiving of Hezekiah for his recovery: 'Sheol cannot praise thee, death cannot celebrate thee; they that go down into the pit cannot hope for thy truth. The living, the living, he shall praise thee, as I do this day.'[3] The nature of the existence attributed to these ghost-souls is not quite consistently described, any more than in the parallel case of the Greek Hades. Probably there is present an older stratum of tradition, nearer to primitive ancestor-worship, which ascribes to the shades some measure of self-consciousness and remembrance, with the power of speech and movement, as well as an acquaintance with the affairs of their descendants and an interest in their welfare.[4] But in process of time the ghosts appear to have lost these remaining links with the world of the living; the kingdom of the dead is represented as a land of silence and forgetfulness. 'The dead praise not Jahveh, neither any that go down into silence.'[5] 'His sons come to honour, and he knoweth it not; and they are brought low, and he perceiveth it not of them.' 'Man lieth down, and riseth not: till

[1] I Samuel xxvi. 19.
[2] Ps. lxxxviii. 5.
[3] Isaiah xxxviii. 18–19.
[4] Cf. Charles, *op. cit.*, pp. 39–40.
[5] Ps. cxv. 17.

the heavens be no more, they shall not awake, nor be roused out of their sleep.'[1] Small wonder if the futility of such a purely negative existence led many to deny an after-life altogether. Such was the position of the Sadducees in the New Testament, who taught that there is neither angel nor spirit;[2] and it was an opinion widely held during the last two centuries before Christ. But the emptiness of the popular belief led others, during the same centuries and earlier, to develop a more coherent and satisfying doctrine of immortality.

It seems strange at first sight that the Jews, with their strongly ethical belief in Jahveh, should ever have been able to reconcile themselves to the gloomy heathen eschatology of Sheol. But it has of course to be remembered that the promises of Jahveh were made to Israel as a nation; and during all the centuries of Israel's existence as an independent people the individual was so accustomed to identify himself religiously with his family and his race, that the absence of personal immortality in any effective sense was not felt as a deprivation. He died and was gathered to his fathers; and his life with its interests, material, social, and religious, was continued in that of his descendants. That simple formula served for a long time.[3] But, with the collapse of the national life, the relation between Jahveh and the individual Israelite inevitably became more direct and personal. Religious feeling was intensified and

[1] Job xiv. 12–21. [2] Acts xxiii. 8.

[3] In the case of the Romans, the third great nation mentioned above, it sufficed also during many centuries of their national existence. It is a significant fact, curious to realize, that there is no singular of the word 'Manes'. 'The spirit of a dead Roman', says Dr. Warde Fowler, 'was not thought of as definitely individualized; it joined the whole mass of the Manes in some dimly conceived abode beneath the earth. It is only in the third century B.C. that we first meet with memorial tombstones to individuals, like those of the Scipios, and not till the end of the Republican period that we find the words 'Di Manes' representing in any sense the spirit of the individual departed.' (*Religious Experience of the Roman People*, p. 341.)

deepened under the chastening experiences of the Exile, and just in proportion to the intensity with which the exiles clung to Jahveh was the greatness of their sense of loss in being cut off at death from his presence. At the same time, through the teaching of the Prophets, the Jewish religion became transformed into a pure Monotheism: the god in whose righteousness Israel had trusted was now recognized by them as the God of the whole earth, using the nations of the world for his own purposes. All local limitations being thus removed, it became impossible to believe that even death could sever the bond that united Jahveh and his faithful worshipper. The dawning of this new confidence may be traced in a few of the Psalms, and there are glimpses of it in the agonized wrestlings of Job. 'The fool and the brutish person perish', writes one of the Psalmists, 'they are appointed as a flock for Sheol. But God will redeem my soul from the power of Sheol: for he shall receive me.'[1] And in the 73rd Psalm a still fuller note is struck. The writer has been wrestling, he tells us, with the problem of the insolent prosperity of the wicked, and it had gone near to undermine his faith in a righteous God. 'Verily [he had been inclined to say], verily I have cleansed my heart in vain, and washed my hands in innocency. For all the day long have I been plagued, and chastened every morning.' But he rises above his doubt, and above the very idea of material reward; and the fresh experience of the divine fellowship, after his temporary doubt and estrangement, inspires an outburst of confident hope: 'Nevertheless, I am continually with thee: thou hast holden me by my right hand. Thou shalt guide me with thy counsel, and afterward receive me to glory. Whom have I in heaven but thee? And there is none upon earth that I desire beside thee. My flesh and my heart faileth: but God is the strength of my heart, and my portion for ever.' No-

[1] Ps. xlix. 10, 14, 15; Cf. also Pss. xvi and xvii.

where in the Old Testament do we find a clear and definite doctrine of immortality. If we think we do in certain passages, it is because we read our own ideas into the language. All that we find is scattered anticipations, vaticinations of the heart, as in this Psalm and a few others. But the importance of these isolated passages is that they indicate the path along which a fuller and more assured belief was eventually reached. They are all inspired by the idea of God as the supreme reality, and the possibility of communion with Him. In his own experience of communion with God, the author of the 73rd Psalm intimates, he has already tasted eternal life. He has been in touch with that from which nothing hereafter can separate him, so that with God his future is secure. It is the nature of his present experience which is the ground of his 'for ever'. Through union with that which is eternal he is himself lifted out of the flux of time.[1]

We may find in the sequel that this is the only fruitful way of approaching the question of immortality. It has at least a remarkable parallel in the religious thought of Greece. Amid an extraordinary divergence in the form and the accompaniments of its manifestation, the first religiously based belief in immortality is reached there along a similar path. The Greek Hades in its main features closely resembles the Hebrew Sheol. It is

[1] Baron von Hügel has stated the point admirably in his recently published *Essays and Addresses on the Philosophy of Religion*: 'The soul, *qua* religious, has no interest in just simple unending existence, of no matter what kind or of a merely natural kind. The specifically religious desire of Immortality begins, not with Immortality, but with God. The religious soul does not seek, find, or assume its own Immortality; and thereupon seek, find, or assume God. But it seeks, finds, experiences, and loves God; and because of God, and of this, its very real though still imperfect intercourse with God . . . it finds, rather than seeks, Immortality of a certain kind. The very slow growth of the belief in Immortality among the Jews . . . was entirely thus—not from Immortality of no matter what kind to God, but from God to a special kind of Immortality' (p. 197).

also the common abode of the departed without regard to moral distinctions. According to the official religious tradition of Greece, a few great criminals, those, namely, who had been guilty of offences against the Olympians, are punished in Tartarus, while a few heroes who were personally related to the gods, by descent or marriage, such as Achilles, Menelaus, Heracles, and others, were translated bodily to the Islands of the Blest in the western sea. But the rest of mankind, heroic or unheroic, good and bad, trod the same path to the gloomy realms of Hades and Persephone. The soul here also is the ghostly double of the living man; but, as among the Jews, it is no longer conceived as retaining the faculties which would enable it to carry on in ghostly fashion the functions of the present life. The 'strengthless heads of the dead', as Homer calls them, are witless and feeble things. They have no consciousness or will in the ordinary sense of the word; for these have their seat in the body—in the midriff and the heart—and they perish with the body. Tiresias, in Odysseus's Descent to Hades, is the only exception: 'To him Persephone hath given judgement, even in death, that he alone should have understanding, but the other souls sweep shadow-like around.' They flock together, 'like bats' we are told, with a strange twittering or gibbering noise, incapable either of bliss or woe. The mother of Odysseus gazes vacantly on her own son. Consciousness returns to the phantoms only when they have drunk the sacrificial blood.

Among both the Greeks and the Hebrews, this view of the soul's existence after death appears to be the result of closer psychological reflection on the nature of mental processes and their connexion with bodily functions. The Hebrews arrived at a triple distinction between body, soul, and spirit. Man as we know him in life and action is 'a living soul', and his soul-life is the result of his composite nature as body and spirit, the body being animated by the divine breath, as it is in the Creation story. That being so, the soul or life is extinguished by the separation of body and spirit at death; and the natural consequence is that drawn by the author of Ecclesiastes: 'the dust returns to the earth as it was, and the spirit [the impersonal breath] returns unto God who gave it.' But the tradition of the primitive ghost-soul was too strong to permit this conclusion to be drawn by popular thought; and accordingly we have the strictly inconsistent conception of 'dead souls', phantoms peopling Sheol but devoid of anything that could be called life or consciousness. In Homer the terminology is different, but the result is the same. The Psyche in the Homeric poems has nothing to do with the conscious life while it is in the body, that being connected, as we have seen, with certain bodily organs and functions. It is, one might say, a superfluity in the Homeric psychology of the living man, and maintains itself simply as a relic or 'survival' of the primitive ghostly double. We hear nothing about it till the moment of its leaving the body, when it appears to be identified with the expiring breath, the 'ghost' which is given up.[1]

In the case both of Sheol and of Hades, therefore, the so-called existence of the shades is more a form of words than a reality. It contains no element of value that men should look forward to it. The well-known words which the poet puts into the mouth of Achilles indicate sufficiently the Greek attitude towards this after-life;[2] and, as for the Hebrews, we have seen the horror of revulsion which it breeds in the mind of Job. Along this line,

[1] Cf. Professor Burnet's British Academy paper, *The Socratic Doctrine of the Soul*, p. 14.

[2] 'Nay, speak not comfortably to me of death, O great Odysseus. Rather would I live on ground as the hireling of another, with a landless man who had no great livelihood, than bear sway among all the dead that be departed.' *Od.* xi. 488–91.

therefore, there could be no advance towards a religious doctrine of immortality. The effect of the official faith in Greece was to make the idea of a future life entirely inoperative. As far as possible men put it out of their thoughts, resigning themselves deliberately, either in a mood of quasi-religious submission or in the lighter spirit of a *carpe diem* philosophy, to the narrow compass of the human lot, and endeavouring to snatch what satisfaction they could from the brighter aspects of the present life.

This temper of mind is reflected in the sepulchral reliefs and inscriptions of classical Greece. The passage in Goethe's *Italienische Reise* is well known, in which he describes the impression made upon him by those he saw at Verona. 'Here is no knight in harness, on his knees, awaiting a joyful resurrection. The artist has, with more or less skill, presented to us only the persons themselves, and so made their existence lasting and perpetual. They fold not their hands, gaze not into heaven; they are on earth, what they were and what they are. They stand side by side, take interest in one another, love one another; and that is what is in the stone, even though somewhat unskilfully, yet most pleasingly depicted.' So, after all that has been brought to light since Goethe's day, Dr. Farnell tells us that, apart from the tomb reliefs connected with actual hero-worship, 'the other grave scenes are usually reticent concerning the faith of the living. The greatest of all this class of monuments, the Attic grave-reliefs of the fifth and fourth centuries, . . . do not attempt, or scarcely at all attempt, to show the life of the after-world, but rather scenes of the grace and loving-kindness of the earthly family life.' Similarly, 'until the middle of the fifth century was passed, the writing on the graves is entirely silent concerning a post-humous existence. The dead person speaks only of this life, his city, his family, clan or children, and often of his own achievement, with pride or with love. . . . The yield of grave-epitaphs from the fourth and third centuries B.C. is still comparatively scanty, and still fewer are those that convey any ardent hopes or positive conviction concerning the future world. . . . The greater number by far of those that express any eschatologic theory or hope at all belong to the later periods of Paganism.'[1] But although this was the natural result of the official faith, the more primitive practices connected with the tendance of the dead persisted widely in ancient Greece,[2] and kept alive a simpler spirit of natural piety. The desire for a real existence beyond the grave had not been quenched.

Few surroundings might seem less promising for the growth of a deeper sense of the future life than the madness into which the Maenads worked themselves, dancing in wild procession through the mountains at midnight, in strange garb, with blazing pine-torches, shrill music, and strange cries, till their frenzy culminated in tearing a living victim limb from limb and partaking of the warm flesh and blood. Yet this Phrygio-Thracian cult of Dionysus, which swept over Greece in post-Homeric times, inspired Euripides with the magnificent lyrics of the *Bacchae* and gave us one of Sophocles's finest odes; and there is general agreement among scholars and anthropologists that just in this wild 'enthusiasm' or possession by the god, this 'ecstasy' in which the individual seems to pass out of himself and feel himself one with the god whose rites he is celebrating, lay the germ of a new conception of the soul and its destiny.

[1] Farnell, *Greek Hero Cults and Ideas of Immortality*, pp. 394-9.

[2] For example, the family meals offered to the dead, at which the departed was regarded either as the host or as an invited guest. So also the Athenian All Souls' Day, which terminated the festival of the Anthesteria. Cf. Farnell, *op. cit.*, chap. xii, 'The Cult of Ancestors', pp. 345, 352.

The fundamental principle of the Olympian religion, as we may call the popular faith of Greece, was the gulf fixed between gods and men, between the 'immortals', as the former are currently designated, and mortal men. 'Mortal things befit a mortal,' says Pindar; 'mortal thou art, cherish only mortal aspirations.' So again, 'Strive not thou to become a god.' 'It behoveth to seek from the gods things meet for mortals, knowing the things at our feet and to what lot we are born. Desire not, thou soul of mine, life of the immortals, but drink thy fill of what thou hast and what thou canst.' Such passages give the keynote of the old Greek ethics and religion, rooted as they are in 'willing resignation to the limitation of human capacity and of human claims to happiness and power, all as essentially different from the life and lot of the world of the gods'.[1] The attempt on the part of mortals to overpass these limits is the offence which most surely calls down upon itself the vengeance of the gods. But in the orgiastic worship of which we have been speaking all this is changed. The underlying idea, the whole aim of the ritual, is the identification of the worshipper with the god; and this is achieved in the moments of divine madness or ecstasy in which he seems literally 'out of himself', a partaker for the time of the eternal being of the god whose history is mystically rehearsed in the ritual. Reflection on this ecstatic mystical experience suggests a very different view of the relation of soul and body from that of hitherto current belief. That which is capable of union with the god must be itself of divine origin, and may be expected to pass after death to its native sphere. This is the central idea of the Orphic religious brotherhoods, whose mysteries became such a powerful factor in Greek life and thought in the sixth century B.C.

[1] Rohde, *Psyche*, ii. 2.

The figure of Orpheus himself is enveloped in myth and legend, but the main fact of his connexion with the worship of Dionysus seems placed beyond reasonable doubt by the legend of his tragic death at the hands of the Thracian Maenads, however we may interpret the details of the story.[1] Certain it is that Orphism adopts what we have found to be the fundamental idea of the Dionysiac enthusiasts, and draws conclusions from it which have profoundly influenced subsequent philosophy and religion. And the point I set out to emphasize was that here, as in the case of the Hebrews, when the idea of immortality in any living sense emerges, it is based on a unique experience. The Dionysiac setting seems remote enough from our ordinary conceptions of religious emotion, but it was at all events, for the participant, a supreme experience in which he felt his whole being as it were merged and consummated. The hope of immortality accordingly did not mean for him simply a desire for the continuance of his ordinary day-to-day life and its activities, but rather the leaving of these behind for a fruition unimaginable save for the actual experience in question. The blessed life hereafter is the consequence or continuation of a communion with the god which the worshipper has already enjoyed.

Central in Orphic religion, along with the belief in the essential divinity of the soul, is the idea of impurity, guilt or sin, as the explanation of its present state. The consciousness of sin, it has been remarked, is, on the whole,

[1] Miss Harrison, who treats him as an historical character, suggests that it may be a record of the resistance he met with from the original votaries of Dionysus in his efforts to soften and humanize their savage ritual. Others regard Orpheus here as a double of Dionysus himself, and Dr. Farnell concludes that the manner of his death may be taken as an example of the form of ritual so familiar to us in the *Golden Bough*, the killing of the priest who temporarily incarnates the god (*Cults of the Greek States*, v. 106).

singularly absent from the public religion of Greece. 'In the Iliad or the Odyssey sin is always objectively regarded, being identified with the spirit of insolence or pride that seeks to transgress the golden law of moderation and encroach upon the rights of others, be it our fellow-creatures or the gods. It is an error of the intellect rather than of the will, for it springs from intellectual blindness or infatuation; and the ultimate responsibility is usually laid at the door of the gods. In the Orphic religion, on the other hand, the subjective aspect of sin becomes more prominent. It is on account of defilement contracted in our pre-natal state that we are exiled from the society of Heaven; and the soul, while present in the body, is fully conscious of this fact. There is no attempt to shift the responsibility elsewhere; the guilt is our own and we must expiate it. "I have faced the penalty for deeds unjust," so speaks the soul when she has finished her pilgrimage, "and now I am come as a suppliant to noble Persephone, beseeching her to be gracious and to send me into the abodes of the pious".'[1] The appeal of Orphic religion may be said to depend entirely on this sense of sin or impurity. Orphism taught a Fall of the soul from its first estate, and the whole object of the Mysteries and of the rules of life there laid down was to point out the way of salvation or release (λύσις). *Διόνυσος λύσιος* was the helper invoked, and those who availed themselves of the proffered aid, and faithfully observed the system of purifications enjoined, were assured of final deliverance from the clogs of mortality and re-admission to the divine life from which they had fallen. It is to Orphism that we owe the play upon words familiar to us in Plato, *σῶμα = σῆμα*. The body is the tomb or prison-house of the soul: what we call life here is really the death of the soul, and the true life of the soul

[1] Adam, *Religious Teachers of Greece*, p. 111.

will be realized only when it is finally delivered from what St. Paul calls 'the body of this death'. Many of the Orphic precepts or rules, as they have filtered through to us, doubtless had in view merely ceremonial impurity or pollution. The taboo on eggs and beans, for example, was due to the fact that these formed part of the usual offerings to the chthonian deities, the gods and spirits of the underworld.[1] But the spirit of Orphic religion passed beyond such ritual observances: the ὁσιότης, the holiness or purity after which it strove, included ethical purity and the religious direction of the life as a whole. Deliverance will not come at the end of the present life: it is not so easy to escape from the cycle of births and deaths to which the soul is condemned by the impurity which clings to it. This inherited and acquired impurity must be expiated in successive incarnations, but deliverance is in the end attainable by the faithful soul.

The golden tablets recently found in tombs in the south of Italy and in Crete are of singular interest as containing a clear expression of the cardinal doctrine of Orphic faith —the divine origin of the soul. Like the Egyptian Book of the Dead, they provide believers with careful instructions as to the route of the soul through the underworld, the dangers to be avoided, and the formula in which they must address Persephone and her servants.[2] 'On your left', we read for example, 'you will find a stream, and near it is a white poplar. Go not near that stream: but you will find another, cool waters flowing from the lake of memory, and by it are guards. Say to them, "I am a child of earth and of starry Heaven, but my race is of Heaven alone. Ye know this well yourselves." . . . And, thus addressed, of themselves they will give thee to

[1] Rohde, *Psyche*, ii. 12.

[2] A full account of these tablets will be found in Miss Harrison's *Prolegomena to the Study of Greek Religion.*

drink from the holy well-spring.' The avowal of origin constitutes the claim to drink of the cleansing water and is doubtless a fragment of some Orphic liturgy. In other tablets the soul presents itself before Persephone with a similar claim, and also as one who has been initiated into the Mysteries and has duly performed all their ritual of purification: 'Out of the pure I come, pure Queen of them below. . . . For I also avow me that I am of your blessed race. . . . I have flown out of the sorrowful weary wheel. . . . I have paid the penalty of deeds unrighteous, and now I come a suppliant to holy Persephone, that of her grace she receive me to the seats of the hallowed.' And the answer comes: 'Happy and blessed one, thou shalt be god instead of mortal.'[1]

The influence of Orphic ideas of the origin and destiny of the soul appears in the poems of Pindar, in the first half of the fifth century B.C., as well as in the verses of the philosopher Empedocles. So far as the poetic machinery of Pindar's Odes is concerned, he draws entirely on the traditional legends of the gods and heroes. The poetry is splendid, but the theology and the moralizing are archaic and conventional, as in the passages which I have already quoted. But certain verses, which strike perhaps a more personal note, are obviously inspired by the Orphic faith. One fragment, for example, gives us the divine origin of the soul: 'While the body of all men is subject to over-mastering death, an image of life remaineth alive, for it alone cometh from the gods';[2] and in another, well known from Plato's quotation of it, he teaches the expiation of sin in the underworld and the return of the purified soul to a fresh term of earthly life.[3]

[1] On 'Apulian' vases, also found in Italy, there are representations of the dead in the company of gods and heroes.

[2] Fragment 131.

[3] Fragment 133, quoted by Plato in the *Meno*, 81.

Still more explicitly, in a beautiful passage in the second Olympian Ode, he states the Orphic doctrine, which we find also in Plato, of a threefold probation, after which those who have kept their souls pure pass to the Islands of the Blest. 'Immediately after death the lawless spirits suffer punishment, and the sins committed in this realm of Zeus are judged by one who passeth sentence stern and inevitable; while upon the good the sun shines evermore through equal nights and equal days, and they receive the boon of a life of lightened toil, not vexing the soil with the strength of their hands, no, nor the waters of the sea, to gain a scanty livelihood, but, in the presence of the honoured gods, all who were wont to rejoice in keeping their oaths share a life that knoweth no tears, while the others endure labour that none can look upon. And whosoever, while dwelling in either world, have thrice been courageous in keeping their souls pure from all deeds of wrong, pass by the highway of Zeus unto the tower of Kronos, where the ocean breezes blow around the Islands of the Blest, and golden flowers are blazing, some on the shore from radiant trees, while others the water feedeth; and with garlands thereof they entwine their hands and their brows.' When the life immediately following the present is thus conceived as an intermediate state of reward or punishment, it is obvious that we have passed beyond primitive theories of mere continuance; and accordingly the grey shadow-world of the old Greek Hades, where good and bad were indiscriminately gathered, divides at once of itself into two contrasted realms, the one a place of calm repose or pleasant recreation, the other a grim and terrible region of purgatorial pain. It is, in fact, the familiar contrast of heaven and hell; only that in both cases we have to do with an intermediate state—the interval between one earth-life and another—not with a final state of bliss or woe. But the glowing images in which a poet like Pindar depicts the temporary Paradise are hardly to be distinguished from those in which he clothes the final consummation when the thrice-tested soul returns to its heavenly home.[1]

Unfortunately, human nature being what it is, the more the Orphics elaborated the terrors of the other world, the more they opened the door to superstitious practices by which the ordinary man, without any thought of changing his life, without any true ethical purpose at all, sought to buy absolution for his sins and thereby evade their consequences. Plato, in a scathing passage of the *Republic*, describes the disreputable practices which Orphic doctrine was invoked to cover in his own day by 'quacks and soothsayers who flock to the rich man's doors and try to persuade him they have a power at command which they procure from heaven, and which enables them by sacrifices and incantations . . . to make amends for any crime committed either by the individual himself or by his ancestors, and that, should he desire to do a mischief to any one, it can be done at a trifling expense, whether the object of his hostility be a just or an unjust man; for they profess that by certain invocations and spells they can prevail upon the gods to do their bidding. . . . And they produce a host of books written by Musaeus, and Orpheus—which form their ritual—persuading not individuals merely, but whole cities also, that men may be absolved and purified from crimes, both while they are still alive and even after their decease, by means of certain sacrifices and pleasurable amusements which they call Mysteries: which deliver us from the torments of the other world, while the neglect of them is punished by an awful doom.'[2] But to identify the spirit of Orphism with the abuses of these unscrupulous practitioners in a later age would be no less unjust than to identify Christian doctrine with the promises of the mediaeval

[1] Cf. the beautiful Fragments 129, 130.

[2] *Republic*, 364-5.

pardoners and indulgence-sellers; and it is matter of common knowledge how much Plato's own views of the origin and destiny of the soul owed to Orphic teaching, and how much of the imagery in which he bodied them forth was borrowed from Orphic sources. Nor does he attempt for a moment to disguise these affinities. On the contrary, on each occasion on which he introduces his doctrine of the Soul, he refers to the 'ancient' or 'secret' source of the idea.[1]

We have respectful tributes from other sources to the widespread influence of the Orphic teaching and its elevating tendency. Orphic societies were established in Magna Graecia in the course of the sixth century, and must have spread to Attica and the western Greek world during the fifth and fourth centuries. In an oration delivered in the Athenian law-courts in the fourth century, Demosthenes (or some other leading orator) refers in reverential terms to Orpheus 'who has instituted for us the most holy mysteries and who declares that justice is seated by the throne of God watching all the actions of mankind'.[2] These Bacchic-Orphic societies continued to be numerous and influential down to the last years of paganism under the Roman empire. Plutarch, at the close of the first century A. D., was himself one of the initiated. In a letter of consolation to his wife on the loss of their infant daughter, he consoles her with the hope of a future life, which as members of a Dionysiac brotherhood they had both been taught to cherish, and with the Orphic view that the soul of their dear one, having dwelt in her body for so short a period, had had less chance of contracting the stains of our mortality, and would therefore depart purer to a higher existence.[3] The

[1] So, for example, in the *Phaedo*, 63 and 70, and at greater length in the *Meno*, 81, where the doctrine is introduced for the first time.

[2] Farnell, *Greek Hero Cults and Ideas of Immortality*, p. 387.

[3] Farnell, *op. cit.*, p. 388.

general scope of the Orphic teaching, and the important place it holds in religious history, could not be better summed up than in the sentences with which Dr. Farnell concludes his latest volume on Greek religion:

'It familiarized the world with the conception of the divine element in the human soul, with the kinship between man and God. It quickened this sense by means of a mystic sacrament whereby man's life was transcendentally fused with God's. It raised the religious emotion to a pitch of ecstasy and rapture far above the Hellenic scale. It strongly marked the antagonism between flesh and spirit and preached with insistence the doctrine of purity, a doctrine mainly ritualistic but containing also the spiritual idea of the purity of the soul from the taint of sin. It divorced religion from the State, making it the pre-eminent concern of the individual soul and the brotherhood. Finally, its chief aim and scope was otherworldliness, its mission was the preaching of salvation, of an eschatology based on dogmas of posthumous retribution, purgatory and of a succession of lives through which the soul is tried; and it promised immortal bliss obtainable through purity and the mysterious magic of a sacrament. Alien in origin, alien to the earlier spirit of Hellenism, and always working in the shadow—for none of the later influential schools of philosophy adopted it—it must be reckoned as one of the forces that prepared the way for the inauguration of a new era and a new faith.'

LECTURE III

PRE-EXISTENCE AND IMMORTALITY IN PLATO

The Orphic conception of the origin and destiny of the soul[1] passes into the full light of philosophical discussion in the Platonic Dialogues; and Plato's name is so irrevocably associated with the doctrine of immortality in philosophical and literary tradition, that we shall not easily find a better way of winding ourselves into the heart of the subject than by a consideration of his method of handling the question and the nature of his results.

The first point to note in Plato is the emphatic primacy, as I may call it, attributed to the Psyche or soul in the dialogues, from the *Apology* onwards to the *Laws*. We have seen how, in Homeric and primitive thought generally, the Psyche appears as a shadowy double of

[1] The pre-existence of the soul and the doctrine of transmigration or reincarnation were also fundamental tenets of the religious brotherhood founded by Pythagoras in the south of Italy at the end of the sixth century, and were associated there also with the pursuit of purity by a variety of ascetic practices and ceremonial observances. The inspiration of Pythagoras may have been derived, as Professor Burnet thinks (*Greek Philosophy from Thales to Plato*, p. 40), not from Dionysus and the Orphics, but from the religion of the Delian Apollo, which goes back to 'Aegean' or 'Minoan' times. Dr. Farnell, on the other hand, treats Pythagoras as 'the most powerful champion and apostle of Orphism', and the Pythagorean clubs and secret societies as the 'militant order' of the Orphic faith (*Outline History of Greek Religion*, pp. 83, 89). But the relations between the two movements (if there were two distinct movements) are now obscured for us by the lapse of time. In the sequel, at all events, the Pythagorean brotherhood was no doubt open to Orphic influences operating in the same region, and the terms Orphic and Pythagorean came to be used almost synonymously. But the later Pythagoreans, it is to be noted, when they became a scientific school in the course of the fifth century, dropped altogether the religious and mystical side of their founder's teaching.

the body, of which nothing is heard during the course of life. Now by Socrates and Plato the soul is recognized from the outset as a man's real self, the self at work in all his ordinary knowledge and actions.[1] Hence to 'care for his soul', becomes man's chief concern. This was the message of Socrates to his fellow citizens, as he describes it in the *Apology*: 'I spend my whole time in going about persuading you all to give your best and chiefest care to the perfection of your souls, and not till you have done that, to that of your bodies or your wealth.' And if we turn to the *Laws*, Plato's last message to the world, we find the burden almost in so many words the same: 'Of all the things which a man has, next to the gods, his soul is the most divine and most truly his own . . . and in our opinion he ought to honour her as second only to the gods. . . . We must believe the legislator when he tells us that the soul is in all respects superior to the body, and that, even in life, *what makes each one of us to be what we are* is only the soul.' And in the context Plato deliberately inverts the traditional conception of the soul as the shadowy image of the bodily self; it is the body, on the contrary, that is the eidolon or shadow of the soul. 'Therefore, when we are dead, the bodies of the dead are rightly said to be our shades or images; for the true and immortal being of each one of us, which is called the soul, goes on her way to other gods, that before them she may give an account.'[2] It is the same thought with which Socrates, at the close of the *Phaedo*, turns to reply to Crito's question, 'How shall we bury you?' '"As you please," he answered; "only you must catch me first and not let me escape you." And then he looked at us with a smile and said, "My friends, I cannot convince Crito that I am the Socrates who has been conversing with you and

[1] Cf. Burnet, *The Socratic Doctrine of the Soul.*

[2] *Laws*, 959.

arranging his arguments in order. He thinks that I am the body which he will presently see a corpse, and he asks how he is to bury me".' 'If we ask', says Jowett, 'what is that truth or principle which, towards the end of his life, seems to have absorbed Plato most, like the idea of good in the *Republic*, or of beauty in the *Symposium*, or of the unity of virtue in the *Protagoras*, we should answer, the priority of the soul to the body.'[1] It is almost as if, at the close of his long life, after all that splendid series of metaphysical efforts, he had fallen back on the primal simplicity of conviction with which he started.

In the second place, we may note that the belief in the divinity of the soul of man and its consequent immortality always appears in Plato as a primary religious conviction, independent of the particular and often unconvincing arguments by which he supports it; and, as we have already seen, in all his set expositions of the doctrine, he avails himself freely of Orphic expressions and imagery, which he himself warns us not to take too literally.

The most brilliant account of the pre-existence and heavenly origin of the soul is given in the *Phaedrus*.[2] 'The soul', he begins, 'is immortal, because its very idea and essence is the self-moved or self-moving, that which is the fountain and beginning of motion to all that moves besides. A body which is moved from without is soulless, but that which is moved from within has a soul.' The movements of the heavenly bodies are due, he supposes, to indwelling souls or spirits, and hence their motions are eternal, as contrasted with those of inanimate things set in motion by other things, which have a beginning and an end. Besides these heavenly spirits, 'visible gods', there are the souls destined to be the souls of mortal beings 'no longer so pure as before'. But *nous* or reason is an ingredient

[1] *Dialogues of Plato*, vol. v, p. 120 (2nd ed.).
[2] *Phaedrus*, 245.

in the constitution of all; and therefore they enjoy originally a bodiless existence in the heavenly region, admitted to the vision of eternal truth, beauty, and goodness—that heaven above the heavens which he celebrates in the *Phaedrus*,[1] the world of pure Ideas or Forms, of which our world of time is the broken reflection. For the same reason —because of their rational nature—the souls all pass at first into the human form. Their second incarnation depends on the kind of life they have led in their first earthly period of probation, and each subsequent incarnation is similarly determined by the use made of the preceding life.

But as to how these bodiless souls come to be imprisoned in the body at all, we hardly get from Plato a consistent account. In the *Phaedrus* he explains it by carrying over into the pre-natal state (in the figure of a charioteer with two unequally yoked steeds) his well-known threefold division of the psychical life into the rational or ruling part, the spirited or courageous element (consisting of the more generous emotions, which are the natural allies of reason) and the lower element of desire and appetite. It is through yielding to this lower element that the soul 'loses her feathers', her wings droop, and she sinks to earth.[2] But this threefold division of mental function is obviously (and necessarily) based upon observation and analysis of our actual embodied life; and Plato elsewhere frankly attributes the disturbing influence of the appetites to the connexion of soul with body. Hence it is illegitimate to presuppose such influence before the union of the two. In this respect Plato's account of the Fall can hardly be considered more successful than other attempts to explain the origin of evil by translating a metaphysical or moral necessity into the narrative of an event which happened once upon a time. Plato seems to have realized this himself, for elsewhere he states things differently. In the

[1] *Phaedrus*, 247. [2] 246.

Timaeus he represents soul and body as everywhere united throughout the created universe; and of human souls in particular he says, 'they were implanted in bodies by necessity'.[1]

The details of Plato's account of the future destiny of the soul, in which he gives a wide range to his imagination, differ considerably in different dialogues. The features which occur in one form or another in all the narratives are the judgement after death, the intermediate state of rewards and purificatory punishments, and the return of the souls to earth in a human or animal form determined by the way in which they have conducted themselves in their previous incarnations. Those who appear to be incurable from the enormity of their sins are hurled down to Tartarus, whence they never come forth again. Those, on the other hand, who have been pre-eminent for holiness in their lives and 'who have sufficiently purified themselves with philosophy' are set free from the body altogether and ascend to the heavenly sphere from whence they came. But this is hardly to be accomplished in a single life. The soul of a philosopher, guileless and true, or the soul of a lover who is not without philosophy may attain deliverance at the end of 3,000 years, if thrice in succession they have chosen their lives aright; but, for the majority, a cycle of 10,000 years must be completed before, by the repeated experience of good and evil, they learn eventually to choose the good.[2] Such, in outline, is Plato's eschatology, presented by him always in mythical form, not, therefore, as a demonstrated or exact philosophical conclusion, but as bodying forth certain important ethical and religious ideas.

But we must not forget that Plato's theory of the soul formed part of, or at least had to be adjusted to, a very

[1] *Timaeus*, 42.

[2] *Phaedrus*, 248-9. Cf. Pindar, as quoted above, p. 29.

definite and characteristic metaphysical theory of reality. This metaphysical theory was the outcome of more than a century's speculation on Being and Becoming. In the doctrine of the Ideas or Forms Plato reached (for the first time in the history of thought) the conception of a mode of being which was eternal, not in the sense of persisting changelessly through time—like the motionless being of Parmenides, the 'mindless unmoving fixture' which he derides in the *Sophist*[1]—but in the sense of absolute timelessness. Truths and ideas are not like things, which exist in space and persist through time; they are eternal in the sense that they have no relation to time at all. The essential function of reason or thought, Plato argued, was the formation of general notions, 'proceeding from many particulars of sense to one conception of reason'.[2] That, according to the Socratic teaching, was the path to definition, and to true knowledge of the nature of the things. For the object of such knowledge is not a subjective abstraction in the mind of the knower. True knowledge implies a real object. The conception reveals to us, so to speak, the law of being of the things in question, their nature, the constitution which makes them what they are. This is surely an object, real in another and, Plato adds, in a higher sense than the particular sensible objects in which the 'law' or 'nature' works. The objects of sense-perception are involved in a perpetual flux and they cannot, in strictness, be known as objects at all, save in so far as they exemplify some universal nature; whereas reason discloses to us a world of reality lifted out of the space-and-time element altogether. Up till Plato's day, however abstractly philosophers might describe what they took to be the ultimate reality, they had always conceived it in spatial and material terms. To whatever subsequent criticisms, therefore, Plato's theory may be

[1] *Sophist*, 249.

[2] *Phaedrus*, 249.

open, it was undoubtedly an important philosophical advance to grasp the sense in which reality may be predicated of these bodiless essences—as he expresses it in his impassioned chant in the *Phaedrus*, 'the colourless and formless and intangible essence and only reality, visible to the mind alone who is lord of the soul.'

Plato's philosophy is dominated by the contrast between this eternal world of intelligible reality and the quasi-real world of γένεσις or Becoming, with which we have to do in sense-perception and in the everyday conduct of our lives. The status of the soul is, in a manner, intermediate between the two: it has relations to both worlds. As what we should call a concrete existent, it belongs to the world of γένεσις or time; but in virtue of its rational nature, its 'kinship' is with the Ideas.[1] That is the condition of its coming to know them, and such knowledge is 'the proper food of every soul'.[2] This kinship is in truth the divine Erôs which inspires the philosophical quest of absolute beauty, perfect knowledge, and true virtue. It is the home-sickness of the soul for its native country. But to say that the soul is akin to the Ideas is not to say that it is itself an Idea. Hence Plato intimates plainly enough that, although souls are immortal and indestructible in time, they are not 'eternal' in the sense in which that is true of the Ideas.[3] Yet, by feeding on her proper food, the soul may, as it were, appropriate this absolute content and make the true, the beautiful, and the good the habitual element in which she lives, becoming thus partaker of their eternal nature. 'He whose heart has been set on the love of learning and of true wisdom, and has chiefly exercised this part of himself, that man must without fail have thoughts that are immortal and divine, if he lay hold on truth: and so far as

[1] *Phaedo*, 79. [2] *Phaedrus*, 247. [3] *Laws*, 904.

it lies in human nature to possess immortality [in this higher sense], he lacks nothing thereof.'[1] It is the same note which is struck in the famous passage towards the close of Aristotle's *Ethics*[2] where he exhorts us to put on the immortal as far as in us lies (ἐφ' ὅσον ἐνδέχεται ἀθανατίζειν). 'If, then, reason be divine, compared with man, the life which consists in the exercise of reason will also be divine in comparison with human life. Nevertheless, instead of listening to those who advise us, as being men, to think human thoughts, as being mortal to think mortal things, it behoves us rather, as far as in us lies, to aim at immortality, to do everything to live in the exercise of the highest of our faculties. For, though it be but a small part of us, yet in power and in value it far surpasses all the rest, and indeed this part would even seem to constitute our true self, since it is the sovereign and the better part.' Neither Plato nor Aristotle is thinking in these passages of a future state. What both have directly in view is an eternal or deathless life which can be lived by us here and now, the life of thought which makes us spectators of all time and all existence ('which apprehends things noble and divine', in Aristotle's words), and to which we can raise ourselves, at intervals at any rate, out of the flux of time with its passing interests and distractions.

The realization of such a 'divine' life is regarded by both thinkers, it will be observed, as open only to 'philosophers'; and although that term has a larger sense in Plato and Aristotle than its English equivalent,[3] it inevitably excludes the mass of mankind. For them, Plato

[1] *Timaeus*, 90. [2] *Nic. Eth.*, Bk. X, c. 7.

[3] Cf. Plato's account of the characteristics of the true philosopher, *Republic*, Bk. VI. In the *Phaedrus*, 248, 'the philosopher, or artist, or some musical and loving nature' are grouped together as 'those who have seen most of truth', and distinguished from those who have seen truth in the second degree, represented by a righteous king or lordly warrior, and from the remaining seven grades of insight.

teaches, 'true opinion' and the customary virtue which is built on that foundation, must necessarily suffice: it is the function of a well-constituted state to promote the growth of such true opinions and the practices to which they naturally tend. So far as the practical result is concerned, Plato freely confesses that 'true opinion may be as good a guide to correct action as wisdom'.[1] But the gulf between the two may be measured by the difference of status assigned to the ruling class in the *Republic*, the different scientific and philosophic education which they alone enjoy, and its final fruit in the vision of the Idea of the Good. The outlook of the other classes seems to be limited to 'their station and its duties'. And similarly, for Aristotle, the 'moral' virtues, as he calls them, those 'which are displayed in our relations towards one another', are 'emphatically human affairs'.[2]

For Plato, it will be remembered, the same distinction operates as regards the blessed or divine life in the future. 'Those who have practised the popular and social virtues ... which come from habit and practice without philosophy or reason, are happiest in the round of transmigration; for it is probable that they return into a mild and social nature like their own, such as that of bees or wasps or ants, or, it may be, into bodies of men, and that from them are made worthy citizens. But none except the philosopher or the lover of knowledge, who is wholly pure when he goes hence, is permitted to go to the race of the gods.'[3] Now, if it is only in virtue of his 'philosophy or reason' that the philosopher attains this blessed immortality, as distinguished from the survival which is the lot of every soul, the question readily suggests itself, how much of the philosopher does Plato suppose to survive bodily death and to enter upon this immortality: for the being or nature of any individual philosopher

[1] *Meno*, 97. [2] *Nic. Eth.*, Bk. X, c. 8. [3] *Phaedo*, 82.

includes a good deal more than his purely rational activities.

The question brings us back to Plato's psychology—to his threefold division of the 'parts', faculties, or functions of the soul—which was merely touched upon above in passing. The pre-existence of individual souls in a state of innocence and their subsequent Fall, as narrated in the *Phaedrus* myth, could not be made consistent, we saw, except by attributing to the as yet unfallen soul inclinations or desires which are themselves intelligible only as the result of its union with the body. As already indicated, Plato himself seems to have become aware of this difficulty; and in other and (most of them certainly) later writings, he represents only the rational soul, or part of the soul, as pre-existent and divine in its origin. Thus, in the mythical account of the creation in the *Timaeus*, he distinguishes between 'the immortal principle' of the soul, which comes from God, and 'a soul of another nature which was mortal, constructed within the body, subject to terrible and irresistible affections—first of all pleasure, the greatest incitement of evil; then pain, which deters from good; also rashness and fear, two foolish counsellors, anger hard to be appeased, and hope easily deceived by sense without reason and by all-daring love'. These, 'mingled together according to necessary laws', went to the making of man. The divine principle was located in the head, with the neck placed as an isthmus and boundary between it and the mortal soul. The nobler part of the mortal soul, 'which is endowed with courage and passion', was settled round the heart, 'in order that it might be within hearing of the reason and might join with it in controlling and restraining the desires when they are no longer willing of their own accord to obey the word of command issuing from the citadel'. The baser part of the mortal soul, 'which desires meats and drinks and all things whereof it has need owing to the nature of the body', was placed below the midriff, 'all this region being contrived as a sort of manger for the food of the body; and there the desires were bound down, like a wild animal which was chained up with man, and must be reared with him if a mortal race was to be at all'.[1] Thus God, he says later in the same work, 'gave the sovereign part of the human soul to be the divinity of each'; through its presence 'we are a plant not of an earthly but of a heavenly growth'; it is this which 'raises us from earth to our kindred which is in heaven'.[2] In the *Republic*, the figure of the man, the lion, and the motley many-headed monster, combined in the external semblance of the man, repeats the same threefold division and the identification of the man—'the inward man'—with the rational part.[3] And again, later on, he describes the soul, as we at present see it, as being in a state like the sea-god Glaucus, marred by the action of the waves, encrusted with shellfish and sea-weed and stones. So the soul has been 'marred by its association with the body and by other evils'; but 'if we wish to understand its real nature', 'we ought to fix our attention on one part of it exclusively, on its love of wisdom'.[4]

But if the rational soul alone, or the rational element in the soul, is heaven-descended, it may well seem to follow that that alone will survive the death of the body. Such, as is well known, was the consequence which Aristotle drew in his famous, if enigmatic, doctrine of the Active Reason. For Aristotle the self-consciousness of the individual, as dependent upon memory and its bodily conditions, lapses at death; nothing survives save the impersonal Reason which temporarily made the organism its vehicle. Whether this is the logical con-

[1] *Timaeus*, 69, 70.

[2] *Ibid.*, 90. For the two Orphic phrases cf. *supra*, pp. 27–8.

[3] *Republic*, 588.

[4] *Ibid.*, 611.

clusion of the Platonic line of thought, it is not necessary at this point to determine. Plato certainly did not draw it; he was too deeply committed by the antecedents of his thought and by his whole temperament to an opposite view.

The specific arguments which Plato adduces to prove the immortality of the soul are, for the most part, singularly unconvincing. In one or two instances he has struck out ideas which reappear frequently in later thinkers; but at other times the argumentation impresses a modern reader as frankly fantastic. So it is, for example, with the first argument in the *Phaedo*[1], that everything which has an opposite (e. g. greater and less, just and unjust, sleeping and waking) is generated only from its opposite. A sleeping man awakes, and a waking man goes to sleep: the two states alternate. Hence, as life and death are opposites, Plato argues, they are similarly generated the one from the other; what dies must have been alive, and what is alive must have been dead. In other words, the souls of the dead must exist somewhere, whence they return again into life. If it were not for this rhythmical process, all things would ultimately be reduced to the same state—in which case, 'everything would at last be dead and nothing alive'. Such an argument would never have suggested itself to Plato, had he not previously accepted 'the ancient belief' to which he refers in the context, and had he not accepted also the idea, which goes with it, and which he explicitly states in the *Republic*[2], of a limited supply of souls. So far as the argument goes, it would be possible to prove on the same principles a perpetual alternation between drunk and sober.

Of a similar verbal character is the more extended argument which is treated as finally conclusive towards the close of the same dialogue, namely, that as an Idea

[1] 70-2. [2] 611.

remains eternally the same with itself and can never pass into its opposite (the idea of the even can never become the idea of the odd, 'whiteness' can never become 'blackness'), so the soul, which is the principle of life, can never die. Now life is certainly not death, and nothing can be alive and dead at the same time. In that sense, 'a dead soul'—a dead life—is a contradiction in terms. But such an argument from the eternal self-identity of Ideas or concepts is very far from proving that a thing which is white cannot become black, or that a living being may not die.

Take, again, the argument used in the *Republic*[1] to prove the indestructibility of the soul: 'nothing can be destroyed except by its own proper and specific "evil".' The eyes, for example, are liable to the evil of ophthalmia, the entire body to disease, timber to rot, copper and iron to rust. The specific 'evil' of the soul is wickedness, and therefore, if the soul is destructible at all, it must die of wickedness. But the truth is (Plato goes on to say) that, so far from being fatal to the wicked individual, wickedness kills other people if it can, but seems often to endow its possessor with peculiar vitality. If, then, the soul cannot be killed by its own depravity, nothing else can destroy it. Once more the argument is little better than a play upon words. The metaphor of virtue as the health, and vice as the disease or incurable cancer, of the soul, is used by Plato with fine effect in the *Gorgias* and throughout his ethical teaching. But to transfer it, as is done here, in a literal sense to the world of generation or becoming, of birth and death, of physical cause and effect, we cannot help feeling to be, as I have said, little better than a play upon words.

The argument in the *Phaedrus* (which has already come under our notice)[2] for the priority and eternity of the soul as the self-moved cause of all movement in the universe is, according to Plato's own statement, an argument about soul

[1] 608-11. [2] p. 35 *supra*.

as such, 'the soul divine and human'. It has its root no doubt, at the animistic level, in the contrast between the living being and inanimate things. The former appears to possess an internal principle of movement: it moves about of its own accord, whereas things move only when they suffer an impact from living beings or from other things in motion. But at such a level the distinction can have no bearing on the question of immortality. As it stands in Plato and Aristotle, with a primary reference to the movements of the heavenly bodies, the argument would require to be transformed out of recognition to make it reconcilable with modern physical conceptions. If sufficiently transformed, it might possibly be identified with the cardinal thesis of every idealist or spiritual philosophy, *Mens agitat molem*; *Causae efficientes pendent a finalibus*. But, however transformed, its reference would be to the cosmos as a whole and the divine informing Spirit of which the cosmos is taken to be the manifestation. What may be true in that reference has no necessary application to individual finite souls.

Nor can the pre-existence of individual souls—which is always treated by Plato as the essential condition of their survival—be said to be proved, or even made probable, by the famous argument that all knowledge is recollection of what we knew in a pre-natal state. The ordinary man, on first hearing of this Platonic doctrine, is prone to think of memories of individual happenings in a previous life, such as legend attributed to Pythagoras, or such as Kipling uses so brilliantly in the tale which he calls 'The Finest Story in the World'. But the facts on which Plato builds are quite different, and attention to his real argument has at once a sobering effect. It is the characteristics of necessary truth, as exemplified in mathematical reasoning, which impress him, and which he sets out to explain. Mathematical truths, as soon as we realize them, are seen to be necessary, and we seem to have known them always. Each step in the demonstration has the same self-evidence; and so Socrates is represented, in the *Meno*, as 'eliciting' from a slave-boy, by a series of appropriate questions, a geometrical theorem of which the boy had no previous conscious knowledge, not having been taught geometry. Yet, as 'the answers were all given out of his own head', the steps by which the demonstration is gradually built up seem comparable to a process of 'recovering' or 'recollecting' knowledge which he has somehow always possessed. 'If the truths only required to be awakened into knowledge by putting questions to him,' Socrates concludes, 'the soul must have always possessed this knowledge. And if the truth of all things (for there seems no limit to this process of recovery) always existed in the soul, then the soul is immortal.'[1]

In the *Phaedo*, the *Phaedrus*, and the *Symposium* the argument for pre-existence is presented in a form more familiar to us in poetic tradition—with explicit reference, namely, to the theory of Ideas. It is the Ideas which are supposed to be recalled to mind by the sight of the earthly objects in which they are reflected:

> When on some gilded cloud, or flower,
> My gazing soul would dwell an hour,
> And in those weaker glories spy
> Some shadows of eternity.[2]

The theme both of the *Phaedrus* and of the *Symposium* is, how the soul using sight, 'the noblest of the senses', is led back from the beauties of earth to the heavenly or absolute Beauty—Beauty in itself, or the Idea of Beauty—by participation in which these earthly beauties are what they are; beautiful certainly, but at their fairest only images seen darkly of that perfect and everlasting Beauty. 'Any beautiful thing', he had said in the *Phaedo*,[3] 'is only made

[1] *Meno*, 85, 86. [2] Vaughan, 'The Retreat'. [3] 100.

beautiful by the presence or communication (παρουσία or κοινωνία), or whatever you please to call it, of absolute Beauty. I do not wish to insist on the nature of the communication (on how the communication or participation is effected), but what I am sure of is that it is Beauty (τὸ καλόν) through which all beautiful things are beautiful (ὅτι τῷ καλῷ πάντα τὰ καλὰ γίγνεται καλά).' In the two other dialogues mentioned, this doctrine of the Ideas is presupposed rather than scientifically expounded; it is applied with mystical fervour as an instrument of ethical and religious regeneration. In the *Phaedo*, which is earlier, there is a short exposition at a more prosaic level, which enables us to understand better the line of thought along which Plato was led to the theory. His examples are abstract mathematical conceptions, such as equality. We pronounce two objects to be equal (in size or height or some other quality). They do in fact appear to us to be equal, and roughly, or for practical purposes, they are so. Yet they only approximate to what we mean by perfect equality; they are aiming at it, Plato says, but they do not actually realize it. The objects *suggest* the idea of equality, he goes on to say, but they do not *give* us the idea, for it is not contained in the sensible facts as we perceive them. The idea is rather the standard by which we judge the facts. 'We must, therefore,' he concludes, 'have had knowledge of equality before we first saw [so-called] equal things, and perceived that they all strive to be like equality and come short of it.'[1] Such knowledge is independent of all sense-experience; we must have received it, therefore, before we were born. And the same holds, he adds, of 'all that we call real', as distinguished from the appearances of sense.

There can be no doubt that Plato is here working out a very important philosophical distinction, and he is

[1] *Phaedo*, 75.

profoundly right in the stress he lays on the ideal concepts of reason and the impossibility of deriving them from passively apprehended data of sense. Concepts are not passively given, they are actively constructed, and on the power to frame them depends the possibility of science. But it is one thing to emphasize the presence and function of reason in experience, and quite another to explain that activity by supposing its products to be given to the individual mind in a prenatal existence. The capacity to frame an abstract idea, and thereby to carry the process of idealization beyond the limits of actual sense-experience, is a qualitative distinction of human intelligence as such, but this capacity has no direct bearing on the duration of the individual human mind, whether as regards pre-existence or a future life.

In his argument from the *unity* of the soul—the only one remaining to be mentioned—Plato's thought is more on the lines of subsequent discussion. The idea of the simplicity or unity of the soul, as contrasted with the multiplex and composite character of the body, has been, down to the time of Kant, if not later, one of the chief philosophical arguments for immortality. It is stated by Plato in the *Phaedo* (78-81), where he bases it on the affinity of the soul to the Ideas. In virtue of that kinship, the soul may be supposed, he argues, to be characterized by the same unchangeable self-identity as belongs (we have already seen) to every Idea as such. The reference to the abstract self-identity of the Ideas gives the argument a different setting from that given to it later in the orthodox tradition of the schools; but the inference from unity or simplicity to indestructibility is common to both, and the contrast in this respect between the unity or simplicity of the soul and the multiplicity of the body is similarly emphasized. Plato mentions the argument again, towards the close of the *Republic*; but he has not elaborated it farther. As it has played such a considerable part in the subsequent discussion of the subject, it will be more to our purpose to examine it at a later stage in its modern form. The doctrine of transmigration or rebirth which is so prominent in Plato's scheme of things, and which is still so widespread a form of religious belief, we shall also have to consider more fully later on its merits.

What we may call Plato's strictly philosophical or scientific arguments all turn, as we have seen, on the relation of the soul to the Ideas; that is to say, they are essentially arguments drawn from the nature of knowledge. Some of these arguments we found to be vitiated by verbal fallacies. In others, where he may be thought to achieve some measure of success, it must be admitted, as Jowett has remarked, that 'in proportion as he succeeds, the individual seems to disappear in a more general notion of the soul; the contemplation of ideas "under the form of eternity" takes the place of past and future states of existence'.[1] The same thing happens with modern arguments based on the constitution or necessary conditions of knowledge; it inevitably happens in any purely epistemological argument. We are left with the abstract unity of consciousness in general, which is realized indifferently in each individual thinker but contains nothing to distinguish individuals one from another or from a so-called absolute or universal consciousness. With Plato, this result may be said to follow necessarily from his conception of philosophy or dialectic as concerned solely with the eternal or unchanging, while the world of time or becoming constitutes the sphere of opinion or probability. Philosophy, so far as it is scientific or exact—so far as it is *knowledge*—is for him an exposition of the eternal nature or structure of reality. It is confined to a statement of universal principles or

[1] Introduction to the *Phaedo* (*Dialogues*, i. 417).

necessary laws, and has nothing to say about individuals, as such, or the course of their history.[1]

The inherent logic of such a view might seem, therefore, to lead to some such doctrine as Aristotle's theory of the Active Reason, or to his idea of God as the pure Thinker, 'the eternal thinking upon thought'. Hence we find Hegel, whose philosophy is similarly based upon theory of knowledge, and who takes the same view of philosophy as concerned solely with the universal and the eternal, making a determined effort to persuade us that all Plato's statements about immortality must be so construed. He will not have it that a philosopher of Plato's eminence could seriously have in view so commonplace a doctrine as individual survival. And as the Platonic speculations on the subject are all presented in mythical form, he would have us dismiss the myths altogether in forming an estimate of Plato's philosophical position, except where their statements can be shown (as, for example, in the case of the doctrine of Reminiscence) to be translatable into terms of pure reason. It is impossible, however, without doing violence to every canon of sound interpretation, to take Plato's manifold statements on this subject as referring to anything but the question of individual destiny. And if the doctrine of immortality reappears so often, and is given such an important place, we cannot be justified in leaving it out of account merely because it is put forward in the course of a professedly mythical narrative. Plato's myths form too important a feature of his philosophical work to be set aside in this summary fashion. If his real position had been what Hegel would have us believe it was, why should he not have been content, as Aristotle was, to confine himself to a strictly scientific treatment? Why did he so often, at a certain stage of his argument, deliberately turn from science to mythology? The Myth, it has long been

[1] Cf. Professor Webb, *Divine Personality and Human Life*, p. 256.

acknowledged, is an essential element of Plato's style, and his philosophy cannot be understood apart from it.

The first step towards a proper understanding of the function of Plato's myths is to perceive that they are not employed merely as a rhetorical or poetical adornment of the discourse, nor yet as an allegory or parable which represents, in deliberately chosen and transparent symbols, a doctrine or body of truth which the author is expounding at the same time in conceptual or scientific form. Plato often uses allegory also (the allegory of the Cave in the *Republic* will occur to every one), but the Myth is on a larger scale, and is intended to be taken and enjoyed in the first instance as a story for its own sake. We do not think, step by step, of the meaning or moral as we go along: it is only the cumulative effect of the narrative as a whole that gives us a vision of the ethical or religious truth it is intended to convey. But this truth, as I have already indicated, is not something which Plato is himself prepared to state in scientific form; it is not anything which he would assert that he *knows* in that sense.[1] The truth, we may say, is rather a vaticination, a prophetic utterance, a fundamental conviction, which he cannot justify or even explain in detail, and which he clothes for that reason in the traditional imagery of the Mysteries. It follows from this that he allows himself complete freedom or poetic licence in regard to the details of the story; he ridicules the idea of these being taken for literal truth by any man of sense. But he is equally emphatic that in its general outline 'either this or something like it is true'. That is what he says in the *Phaedo*[2] at the end of his story about 'the soul and her habitations', and it is the principle which we must apply to all his myths,

[1] Cf. Zeller, *Plato*, p. 161 (English translation): 'The Platonic myths almost always point to a gap in scientific knowledge.'

[2] 114 D.

if we are to interpret them intelligently. It is only the central idea of the tale which he is prepared to stand by—in this particular case, the idea of the continued existence of individual souls under a system of moral order and discipline.

I remarked, in speaking of Orphic religion, that in it we had passed beyond theories of mere continuance; the doctrine of a future life had become definitely associated with ideas of 'retribution', or, as we might put it more broadly, with the idea of a moral government of the world. This idea constitutes, in fact, from henceforth the real significance of the doctrine; and in the general mind the idea of a moral order or government of the world takes the form of a belief in the systematic distribution of rewards and punishments after death for the deeds done in the body. So expressed, the belief often assumes crude and questionable shapes; and it has been frequently attacked as fundamentally unethical in its presuppositions, and subversive of the very morality which it professes to vindicate. As Plato introduces the idea of rewards and punishments freely in all his eschatological myths, often using the imagery of religious tradition, it is of some importance that we should not misconceive his real position in this matter. We may begin by recalling the scornful mirth he makes in the *Republic* of the religious teachers who describe the righteous dead 'as reclining on couches at a banquet of the pious, and with garlands on their heads spending all eternity in wine-bibbing, the fullest reward of virtue being in their estimation an everlasting carousal'.[1] It is the same note of indignant scorn with which Spinoza turns upon 'those who expect to be decorated by God with high rewards for their virtue and their best actions, as for having endured the direst slavery—as if virtue and the service of God were not in itself happiness and perfect freedom'.[2]

[1] *Republic*, 363.

[2] *Ethics*, II. 49 Sch.; cf. V. 41 Sch.

The disinterestedness and the self-sufficingness of virtue is the central text of Plato's ethics, to which he returns in dialogue after dialogue. Virtue is 'the health of the soul', 'the right constitution' or ordered harmony of our nature. It is, in short, the realization by man of his true nature, and only in realizing its own nature can any being achieve happiness. To inquire, therefore, whether virtue is 'expedient', whether goodness is 'profitable', is to perpetrate an abuse of terms. As well ask, he says, whether it is better to be sick or to be well, to be a marred and useless soul or a soul that is capable and strong, whether it is better to subject the human and divine element in our nature to the animal or the animal to the divine. The metaphors are various, but the thesis is everywhere the same. Spinoza gave it immortal expression in the closing proposition of his *Ethics*: *Beatitudo non est virtutis praemium sed ipsa virtus*, which we may perhaps paraphrase: 'A blessed life is not the reward of goodness but the practice and enjoyment of goodness itself.' The reward which the good man looks for is nothing extrinsic, to be conferred upon him, but only, in Plato's phrase, to become like God as far as man may.[1] And, as goodness is its own reward, so the evil life carries its own penalty with it. 'The true penalty of wrongdoing', he says in a well-known passage of the *Theaetetus*, 'is one that cannot be escaped. There are two patterns eternally set before men, the one blessed and divine, the other godless and wretched; and, in their utter folly and infatuation, [the evil doers] do not see that they are growing like the one, and unlike the other, by reason of their evil deeds: and the penalty is that they lead a life answering to the pattern which they resemble.'[2]

The good life therefore stands unassailable in its own strength, and the belief in immortality is not based by Plato on the ordinary argument from the need for com-

[1] *Republic*, 613. [2] *Theaetetus*, 176.

pensation and retribution. He is in fact careful, at the close of the *Republic*, before he begins the story of Er, to call Glaucon's attention to the fact that such extrinsic sanctions as he there describes are being brought in, and can legitimately be brought in, only after the demonstration that righteousness is, as he has been arguing in the immediately preceding context, the health and highest good of the soul, just as wickedness is its proper disease, and that righteousness, therefore, is to be desired for itself alone. But it seems natural to him that, in the universe of a good God, the just man will be 'dear to the gods' and the object of their special care, so that 'all things will work together for good to him in the end, either in this life or in another'. 'For unquestionably', he says, 'the gods can never neglect a man who determines to strive earnestly to become righteous, and by the practice of virtue to become as like God as man is permitted to do.'[1] And it seemed to him also natural, in such a world, that, with a view to their eventual reformation, the wicked should suffer the penalties of their misdeeds which they had escaped on earth. Moral principles work themselves out there as here. The important point is the continuity of the future life with the present, and the conviction that the purpose of the whole is good. Plato's belief in immortality is ultimately grounded, therefore, in the central tenet of his theology, the belief that God is good, and that the End of the intelligent creature is likeness to God, so far as that is possible under human conditions. Hence the horizon of such a life cannot be limited by the grave. The good man goes to meet death confident that in the life beyond he will find himself in the same divine fellowship to which he has been admitted here.

But Plato does not claim that even this supreme conviction as to the nature of God and the divine government of

[1] *Republic*, 612–13.

the world is matter of necessary knowledge, like a logical or mathematical theorem, or that it can be explicitly ascertained to be true, as we establish the occurrence of a particular event or the existence of a particular object at a definite time and place. And that is why he frequently presents the Idea of God (as well as the doctrine of the Soul and its destiny) in a mythical form—not because it is not foundational for his whole system of belief, but because it is not science in the sense in which he uses the term. It is, as I have called it, a supreme conviction—faith or belief, as distinguished from demonstration or intuitive truth; but it is a conviction or faith on which a man must be prepared to hazard all he has and is. His life must be ordered on the assumption of its truth. Similarly, the idea of immortality is presented in the *Phaedo* as a great hope, a glorious venture (ἡ ἐλπὶς μεγάλη, καλὸς ὁ κίνδυνος).

The two Ideas (of God and Immortality) are often interwoven in Plato's statements; and in both cases it is noteworthy that what he is concerned to insist upon is the practical lesson to be drawn from the belief for the conduct of life. That is characteristic of the whole position. The existence of God and the immortality of the Soul are not treated by Plato as part of a scientific theory of the unseen world, but primarily as regulative Ideas for the direction of our life here and now. We are to act throughout *as if* they were true. For Plato, it is not too much to say, the practical meaning of immortality is just the infinite importance of right action. The strong resemblance between Plato's attitude and Kant's doctrine of the Ideas of the Reason as regulative principles operative in all our knowledge is illuminatingly insisted on by Professor Stewart in his suggestive book, *The Myths of Plato*, and in this characteristic he finds the true explanation of Plato's preference for a mythical treatment of the doctrines in question.

Undoubtedly the importance of any religious truth consists in its present application to the conduct of life: that is just what distinguishes a religious truth from a purely intellectual theorem. And in the case of the idea of immortality it is very instructive to note how uniformly Plato returns from the imaginative details of his myths, or even from the doctrine itself as a speculative truth, to the practical conclusions to be drawn from the belief. Thus in the *Meno*, where the doctrine is first introduced, Meno hails Socrates's conclusion. 'I feel somehow that I like what you are saying', he remarks; and we can see that it attracts him as an interesting and romantic speculation, of which he hears now for the first time and which he would like to follow out. But Socrates at once discourages such transcendent flights. He will not even put his own conclusion dogmatically: all that he will pin himself to is the practical application to the problem of knowledge and the quest of truth. 'Some things I have said of which I am not altogether confident. But that we shall be better and braver and less helpless if we think that we ought to inquire, than we should have been if we indulged in the idle fancy that there was no knowing and no use in searching after what we do not know—that is a theme upon which I am ready to fight, in word and in deed, to the utmost of my power.' Similarly, after the elaborate myth of the judgement after death, at the close of the *Gorgias*, he turns at once to the practical lesson: 'I, then, Callicles, am persuaded of the truth of these things, and I consider how I shall present my soul whole and undefiled before the Judge in that day. Renouncing the honours at which the world aims, I desire only to know the truth and to live as well as I can, and when I die, to die as well as I can. . . . And I exhort you also to take part in the great combat, which is the combat of life, and greater than any other earthly conflict.' 'And', he concludes, 'of all that has been said, nothing remains unshaken but the saying that to do injustice is more to be avoided than to suffer injustice, and that the reality and not the appearance of virtue is to be followed above all things, as well in public as in private life.' If we turn to the end of the myth in the *Phaedo*, it is the same: 'Wherefore, Simmias,' Socrates proceeds, 'seeing all these things, what ought we not to do, that we may obtain virtue and wisdom in this life? Fair is the prize and the hope great. . . . Let a man be of good cheer who has arrayed his soul in her own proper jewels, temperance and justice and courage and nobility and truth; thus adorned, she is ready to go on her journey to the world below when her time comes.' And once more, in the *Republic*, in the course of the story of Er, Socrates pauses to make the same application.

Such a *catena* of passages might doubtless be extended almost indefinitely, but those which I have quoted are more than sufficient to illustrate my point. They constitute, I think, a striking testimony to the sobriety of Plato's personal teaching on this great question. If we contrast these grave utterances with the playful references, quoted some time ago, to the souls of certain classes of men returning to earth as animals of a mild and social nature, as bees or ants, it is not difficult to distinguish the creed by which Plato lived from the popular religious ideas, familiar to his audience, which he uses, as it suits him, 'to point a moral or adorn a tale'.

In taking leave of Plato for the present, this may be said in conclusion. Unconvincing as most, perhaps indeed all, of his arguments for immortality may seem to us, his personal conviction produces a profound impression and has had the most far-reaching historical influence. His formal arguments may appear to carry us no farther than the abstract eternity of thought, but it was a conscious and individual immortality in which Plato believed. There are many sides to his genius. His philosophy of mathematical science is only now being appreciated at its full value. He was at the same time a social idealist on the grand scale, his two longest works being devoted to sketching the outlines of an ideal commonwealth. But there is also the mystic and ascetic, whose citizenship is in heaven, to whom the body is but the prison-house of the soul, and who defines philosophy as one long 'study of death and dying', seeing that only 'after we are dead can we gain the wisdom which we desire'. The true philosopher is 'in every respect at enmity with the body and longs to possess his soul alone'; he 'longs to be released from the company of his enemy'. Till God releases him, his struggle is to 'live pure from the body, to have no communion or intercourse with it beyond what is absolutely necessary'. In St. Paul's phrase, he 'dies daily' to the body and its affections, that he may attain true knowledge and true virtue. He anticipates the apostle's metaphor when he describes philosophy as 'the practice' (or 'rehearsal') of dying and death. In fact the nearest parallel to the series of passages I have culled from the *Phaedo*[1] is to be found in St. Paul's impassioned call for deliverance 'from the body of this death', his 'desire to depart', 'knowing that, whilst we are at home in the body, we are absent from the Lord'. 'We ought to fly away from earth to heaven as quickly as we can', Plato says again in the *Theaetetus*[2], 'and to fly away is to become like God, as far as this is possible; and to become like him is to become holy and just and wise.' It is not wonderful that the Fathers of the Christian Church recognized in Plato a kindred inspiration.

For myself, however, I should describe this ascetic or mystic flight from the body, and from the whole life we lead

[1] 64, 66–8. [2] 176.

here, as Orphic rather than strictly and in the highest sense Platonic. Plato was deeply influenced by the Orphic tradition, as I have insisted; but still it represents only one phase of his many-sided genius, to some extent, perhaps, a phase which he lived through. The Orphic influence seems to culminate and to find most concentrated expression in the *Phaedo*, from which the expressions I have just quoted are almost entirely drawn. In no other dialogue, if I remember rightly, is true knowledge said to be attainable only after death; in no other is such despite done to the body as to pronounce it the irreconcilable enemy of the soul, all intercourse with which is to be scrupulously avoided, or such indiscriminate censure passed upon the senses as being not helps, but hindrances, in the quest of truth.[1] The beauties of earth are treated elsewhere as an imperfect vehicle, but still a vehicle, of the eternal Beauty. They are the ladder reaching from earth to heaven, on which we mount to the final vision; and, when we have won our way on high, there is no talk of throwing down the ladder by which we ascended. The philosopher is bidden elsewhere[2] to use 'sight the noblest of the senses' as a coadjutor in his task; and the present life, we are taught, can yield 'fair notions and fair practices'—'the beauty of laws and institutions and sciences'[3]—which have their own intrinsic value. We must supplement one dialogue by another, therefore, if we are to gain a correct impression of Plato's spiritual outlook as a whole. By its historical setting and the marvellous beauty and

[1] 'The philosopher is to be set free as far as possible from the eye and the ear, and in short from the whole body, because intercourse with the body troubles the soul and hinders her from gaining truth and wisdom.' 66.

[2] In the *Timaeus*, 47, sight is celebrated as the main source of philosophy, inasmuch as it reveals to us 'the stars and the sun and the heavens', and has thereby given us 'the invention of number and the conception of time and the power of inquiring about the nature of the whole'.

[3] *Symposium*, 210, 211.

restrained pathos of the closing scene, the *Phaedo* has naturally impressed itself more deeply on the memory of the world than any other of Plato's works. But there is a certain sense of strain in its other-worldliness—noticeable perhaps chiefly in the earlier pages—a certain exaggeration of language and sentiment, which is hardly in accord with the large serenity of outlook which remains with us as the dominant characteristic of Plato's temperament and genius.

LECTURE IV

MIND AND BODY

THE Orphic-Platonic doctrine of the Soul depends on ethical and religious considerations. In that sense it resembles a presupposition on Plato's part, rather than the result of his own psychological analysis or of any independent scientific investigation into the actual relation of soul and body. There is in fact, according to this doctrine, no real relation between them; they are treated as two separate and independent entities. The pre-existent soul 'cometh from afar' to be the tenant of a particular body, and any soul may inhabit any body.[1] The belief in the transmigration of a human soul (i.e. of a soul that had been united with a human body) into the body of one of the lower animals places this beyond doubt. But, even if we limit the idea of transmigration to the passage of human souls into other human bodies, the soul is in each case only the temporary inmate or tenant of the particular body. Soul and body belong to two different worlds; and, although the soul is no doubt conceived as conditioned for the time by the nature of its dwelling-house (being dependent on so many avenues of sensation for its knowledge, and so forth), and also as liable to contamination from the desires which have their seat in the body, it is still in its intrinsic nature a creature of another sphere. This dualism is fundamental in Plato's theory, and from him it passed into the orthodox Christian tradition. Plato, as we

[1] Cf. Aristotle, *De Anima*, i. 3, 407 b: 'Most theories concerning the soul attach the soul to, and enclose it in a body, without further determining why this happens . . . just as if it were possible for any soul taken at random, according to the Pythagorean stories, to pass into any body.'

have seen, reverses the primitive animistic conception of the soul as the shadowy double of the body, insisting that the soul is the true self, to which we owe our best care and tendance; but he preserves and accentuates the original animistic dualism. And the same holds true of the Christian tradition. Man is a composite being, whose two constituents are *brought* together, and, as it were, tied together without possessing any organic or inherent relation to one another. But a dualism of this kind seems to be due, I repeat, to the religious preconception of the separate existence of the soul. It is not naturally suggested by dispassionate reflection on the experience open to our observation. Approaching the question with a purely scientific interest, and starting from the biological facts, Aristotle was led to a very different view of the soul and its relation to the body. Naturalistic as it sounds, and naturalistically as it has in the main been understood, it comes, I believe, much nearer to a true theory of the known facts.

Instead of starting, as Plato seems to do, with the undefined idea of the soul, as the term is used in religion and ethics, Aristotle starts with the living organism, and treats conscious experience as the final form or expression of the biological facts. Keeping in view the wide original meaning of the Greek term, he defines the Psyche comprehensively as the principle of life—the principle in virtue of which living beings perform the characteristic functions which distinguish them from non-living things. He is thus led naturally to distinguish different levels of psychical function. The fundamental function, presupposed in all the rest, is the assimilation of nutriment, and the growth and decay of the organism connected therewith. To this nutritive or vegetative soul are added, in an ascending scale, the sensitive soul, as seen in animals—involving sensation or sense-perception with spontaneous motion in space—and, finally, the rational soul, the function of reason or intelligence, found only in man. Each of these successive stages appears as a development from the one preceding, the higher functions having the less highly developed as their basis. With sense-perception go the feelings of pleasure and pain and appetition or desire, which determine the animal's movements, also *φαντασία* or imagination, the faculty of retaining images of past impressions. This passive retention of associated images which automatically recall one another is the stuff of memory. The data of sense-perception and of this automatic memory furnish the material for the higher functions of active recollection, of judgement and reason, as exemplified in human life. Sensations, images, and the associations which arise between them at the sentient level are transformed by thought into the knowledge of a world of objects. For Aristotle, as for Plato, the essential function of reason is the framing of the concept or, as Aristotle puts it, the apprehension of the universal. On this power of abstraction all reasoning depends: it alone gives the possibility of science. Aristotle did not separate the intelligible world from the sensible, as Plato's language makes us think Plato is doing; but he insists, as strongly as his master, on this thought-world, 'visible to the mind alone which is the lord of the soul'. For Aristotle, as it has been well put, 'the world of abstractions and ideals is not a world of prototypes of which the actually existing things are a kind of reflection or distortion, but is a conceptual world, sublimated from the world of sense and experience, not existing in itself apart from things, but existing for the mind in things.' [1]

Aristotle's technical definition of the soul, as implied in these various functions, depends on the fundamental distinction between matter and form, or the potential and the

[1] P. H. Wicksteed, *Reactions between Dogma and Philosophy*, p. 11.

actual, a distinction which determines his whole philosophy. These are the two aspects of every concrete being. In this case the living being, or, as Aristotle phrases it, 'the natural body possessing or sharing in life', is the concrete unit under investigation, and body and soul are the two correlative terms by which we explain or formulate the characteristic mode of its existence. We may not identify the living being with the body, because the natural body is only the potentiality of life. The soul is the actualization of that potentiality, or, according to the other antithesis, the body is to be looked at simply as the material, the condition or set of conditions, for the expression of the soul or form. The soul is, therefore, technically defined by Aristotle as the Entelechy, the realization or actualization of that life which the organized body possesses in potentiality. The soul is the 'fulfilment'[1] of the body, the end for which the body exists. If we are to apply the predicates unity and reality, it is to the Soul as Entelechy, Aristotle says, that they are peculiarly applicable.[2]

Body and soul are thus not two separate entities; still less can any soul inhabit every body. Each soul is the soul of such and such a body, and each body the seed-plot of such and such a soul. And, according to Aristotle's dominant mood and his usual form of statement, the idea of a disembodied or discarnate soul seems almost a contradiction in terms. For matter and form are, as we began by saying, simply two aspects of the one concrete being (the man, in this case) which alone really exists. If we take the word in its largest sense, the soul for Aristotle is the *functioning* of the body, and he himself gives the analogy of an axe. Cutting is the proper function, or, as it were, the soul of the axe; but we never imagine 'cutting-

[1] Cf. Wicksteed, *op. cit.*, p. 428, 'goal-fulfilment.'

[2] Τὸ γὰρ ἓν καὶ τὸ εἶναι ἐπεὶ πλεοναχῶς λέγεται, τὸ κυρίως ἡ ἐντελέχειά ἐστιν. *De Anima*, II. 1. 412 b.

ness' as an entity existing by itself in independence of the steel. 'In the same way,' he adds, 'if the eye were a living being, seeing would be its soul.' As seeing is to the eye, 'so is sensation as a whole to the whole sentient body as such'.

But just at this point Aristotle's statements cease to be entirely consistent. While maintaining the essential correlativity and inseparability of body and soul throughout the lower ranges of soul-experience, he makes the faculty of reason, at least in its highest reaches, an exception to this principle. 'It is not difficult to see', he says, 'that the soul, or certain parts of it, if it is by nature divisible, cannot be separated from the body. There is no reason, however, why some parts may not be separable, if they are not the realization or actuality of any body whatever. Moreover, it is not clear whether the soul may not be the actuality of the body in the same fashion as a sailor is of his ship.' Such is the unexpected conclusion of the chapter on which the account I have given of his theory is based. The last sentence, if taken seriously, would subvert the whole position he has laid down, reintroducing, as it does, the idea, ostensibly discarded, of the soul as the inhabitant of the body, the manipulator of the machine. But Aristotle follows out the line of thought which these sentences suggest only in regard to *Nous*—that is to say, the rational soul. It is at this point that he introduces his much-discussed distinction between the Active and the Passive Reason. 'The human soul is *potentially* intelligent', he tells us; it has the *capacity* of rational knowledge. But, in order that this potentiality or capacity be made actual, there is needed the operation of an active principle. And this intelligence—*Nous* in this sense—is separable and impassive and unmixed, being in its essential nature an activity.'[1]

[1] *De Anima*, Bk. III. 5. The whole passage in which Aristotle states his

The precise meaning of Aristotle's doctrine has been the *crux* of his commentators from his own day till the present. From the language in which he describes its unintermitted thinking, its eternity and its separateness, Alexander of Aphrodisias (about 200 A. D.) identified the Active Reason with the perpetual divine activity (described by Aristotle as the eternal thinking upon thought, the unmoved source of all movement in the universe) by whose operation upon the receptive soul of the individual—the sensitive and imaginative faculties which constitute, as it were, the material of reason—knowledge is actually, but intermittently, realized in this or that individual man. But the extreme transcendence or aloofness of Aristotle's God makes it difficult to believe that such an identification can have been in his mind. Avicenna and Averroes, the Arabian commentators so well known to students of Aristotle in the Middle Ages, identified the Active Reason not with God but with the guiding intelligence of the lunar

point and draws his conclusions is so short that it may be given in full: 'But since, as in the whole of nature, to something which serves as matter for each kind (and this is potentially all the members of the kind) there corresponds something else which is the cause or agent, because it makes them all (τὸ αἴτιον καὶ ποιητικόν, τῷ ποιεῖν πάντα), the two being related as art to its material—these differences must necessarily be found in the soul. So to the one intellect, which answers to this description because it becomes all things, corresponds the other because it makes all things, just as light, in a manner, converts colours which are potential into actual colours. And this intellect is separable and impassive and unmixed, being in its essential nature an activity. For that which acts is always superior (τιμιώτερον) to that which is acted upon, and constitutes the cause (ἀρχή) of the matter. Now actual knowledge is identical with the thing known, but potential knowledge is prior in time in the individual, though not in the universe at large. The active intellect does not think at one time and at another time not think. Only in separation from matter is it what it really is, and this [its essential nature] is alone immortal and eternal. But *we* do not remember, because the reason of which we are speaking (τοῦτο) is impassive, while the intellect which can be affected (ὁ δὲ παθητικὸς νοῦς) is perishable, and without the former (τούτου) does not think at all.'

heaven—that is to say, the lowest of those planetary spirits in which both Plato and Aristotle believed. Averroes, introducing a further distinction between the passive or passible intellect, which is part of the individual soul, and the Potential Intellect,[1] which is realized in the individual through the operation of the Active Reason, declared the Potential Intellect also to be 'separate', and to be, in fact, single or identical in all men. Such a doctrine seems to abolish human personality altogether, so far as intellect or rational thought is concerned. But, as we are safe in saying that Aristotle had not formulated for himself the conclusions drawn from his statements, either by Alexander or by the Arabians, we need not enter further into the controversy here. It is sufficient to note that Aristotle's doctrine of Reason as an extraneous factor operative in the human consciousness, instead of prompting a belief in individual immortality, leads him personally to a directly opposite conclusion. He speaks of the Active Reason, in another of his books,[2] as coming from without (θύραθεν), 'from out of doors', into the human organism, and as being 'alone divine', phrases almost Orphic in their suggestion. But his actual position is plainly stated in a passage towards the beginning of the *De Anima* (I. 4), where he asserts more loosely of *Nous* in general what he afterwards restricts to the Active Reason. *Nous*, he says, 'would seem to be developed in us as a self-existent substance (οὐσία τις οὖσα) and to be imperishable. . . . But reasoning (τὸ διανοεῖσθαι), love, and hatred are not attributes of the thinking faculty (τὸ νοεῖν) but of its individual possessor, in so far as he possesses it. Hence, when this possessor perishes, there is neither memory nor love: for these never belonged to the thinking faculty, but

[1] Aquinas calls the Passive the Material, and the Potential the Passible, Intellect.

[2] *De Generatione Animalium*, Bk. II. 3. 736 b.

to the composite whole which has perished, while νοῦς is doubtless (ἴσως) a thing more divine and is impassive (ἀπαθές).'

But, however abruptly and unexpectedly it makes its appearance in the context of Aristotle's psychology, this conception of the function of reason, as supervening upon the animal organism and its processes, fitted admirably into the framework of Christian dogmatic. The patristic and scholastic doctrine of the rational soul, as specially created by God and infused into the organism, either at the moment of conception or at a given point in the embryonic history of the foetus, is, so far as the words go, largely a reproduction of Aristotle's statement, although the sense they were intended to convey was in important respects different, and involved a diametrically opposite conclusion. The question with the schoolmen is not, as with Aristotle, of an impersonal function of thought, but of an individual substance 'produced from nothing by the creative act of God'[1] and introduced into the bodily organism. According to scholastic orthodoxy, the soul is not derived, like the body, from its parents. It is 'intrinsically independent' of the body, according to one of the phrases used, although 'extrinsically dependent', in the sense that it enters into relations with the body, and that certain of its activities are correlated with brain states and in that sense dependent on the instrumentality of the organism. But it neither grows nor decays with the body. At most we can say that it gradually unfolds its native capacities, as the development of the brain and nervous system furnishes opportunity. The body is to be regarded throughout as an instrument or means of communication.

Stated thus, however, the theory is on the way to prove too much; and, according to the scholastic habit, so many

[1] M. Maher, *Psychology*, p. 573 (Stonyhurst Philosophical Series).

qualifications are interwoven as we proceed, that a great deal of what seems to be asserted is really withdrawn. For we cannot help pressing the question, *how much* is actually created and imported into the organic conditions. No one, I think, will assert that he himself, as he now exists, was created ready-made at the moment suggested. The ready-made creation of a soul or self in that sense is a transparent absurdity. It makes the whole process of experience superfluous. A self-conscious being can only make itself. If, then, we press our question, the special creation of a rational soul to meet the given circumstances comes practically to mean no more than that the human embryo in question is born with the potentiality of reason, and that this particular body is the means appointed for its realization. The coming into being of the rational soul, or, to put it otherwise, of a self-conscious spirit, is justly regarded as the 'main miracle' of the universe; it has the appearance of being the goal of a divine purpose. The origination and development of such spirits may appropriately, therefore, be spoken of as a creation; for it is the emergence of something new, something which cannot be explained or understood from the conditions out of which it arises, if we think of these conditions as they appear in themselves, apart from the result in which they fulfil and transcend themselves. The soul is regarded by Aristotle as the entelechy or fulfilment, the complete account, of the living body; but, if you think of the body as so much space-occupying matter and no more, it appears to have no relation at all to the living experience which is its ultimate expression. This is characteristic of the process of creative evolution everywhere. The soul, it has sometimes been said, weaves itself a body. From the point of view I am at present emphasizing, we might rather say the body grows itself a soul. The two modes of statement are not ultimately inconsistent with one another, although both are obviously metaphorical. To put the position more prosaically, the organism in commerce with the environment is the medium in which the soul comes into being; and because the organism is a natural body derived from the parents, there are represented in its spiritual product all the influences summarized under the head of heredity.

We require, I think, to follow out Aristotle's conception of the relation of soul and body consistently to the end, applying it, that is to say, to the rational soul no less than to the lower levels of soul-life. Evolutionary process is the fundamental and distinctive conception in Aristotle's philosophy, yet at certain critical points he unexpectedly drops the clue that has served him so far. In the present instance, the larger scope of modern science may enable us to be truer to Aristotle's principle than he was himself. Professor Ward, who certainly will not be suspected of materialistic leanings, remarks that 'but for certain physiological errors into which he fell, Aristotle would doubtless have found the connexion between the organism and the soul as intellectual, more direct, and more definite than he supposed': 'through sensation, phantasy, memory, we advance to recollection, conception, intellection'.[1] In spite of the decisive significance which attaches to the emergence of the conceptual reason—a significance which I have repeatedly emphasized[2]—there is no occasion to contest the conclusion suggested by the scientific history of the globe and of the race, that man attained this faculty by infinitely gradual steps. The qualitative difference between two planes of mind may be profound, and its consequences infinite; yet in the historical process we seem to pass almost insensibly from the one to the other, just as, in traversing a mountain-pass, we may often be

[1] *Psychological Principles*, p. 5.

[2] Cf. *Idea of God*, p. 100 *et seq.*

some way down the farther slope before the welcome trickle of a stream assures us that we have already crossed the watershed. As for the churchly doctrine of a rational soul implanted in each individual organism, by all means let us think of the individual life-history, no less than of the cosmic development, as a divinely directed process, to which, in view of its issue, no fitter word than creation can be applied. But do not let us imagine a divine figure standing by to inject a bit of supernatural stuff into the bodily mixture at the appropriate moment. The soul is no insulated supernatural being, infused into certain extraneous material conditions, but should be recognized as the natural, though not the less divinely ordained, outcome of these conditions themselves.

The idea of the soul as intrinsically independent of the body and only *brought* into relation with it, takes philosophical form in the assertion of the *substantiality* of the soul. Substance means here 'id quod per se stat', a concretely existent thing as distinguished from qualities or attributes which are conceived as existing *in alio*, i.e. as the attributes or activities of some real being. And the definition of the soul as an immaterial or spiritual substance is intended precisely to exclude the possibility of regarding the mental phenomena as attributes or activities of the body. The fundamental argument for the definition is based on the fact that a subject of mental experience is universally assumed and expressed in our ordinary language. Mere sensations or ideas are abstractions of the psychologist: in actual fact they always appear as elements of what we may call a personal life. We shall presently have to consider with some care exactly how much the unity of consciousness (as it is somewhat ambiguously called) amounts to, and how far it carries us. But the traditional definition of the soul as substance undoubtedly betrays us easily into a thinly disguised materialism. The original and natural application of the term 'substance' being, in point of fact, to material bodies possessing mass and other properties, it is difficult to rid ourselves of spatial and material associations. Consequently, although the soul is expressly called by philosophers an 'immaterial substance', it continues to be thought of on the analogy of a physical thing.

The ordinary idea of such a thing implies an ultimate core of reality which remains unchanged throughout the changes of its more superficial states or qualities; and the soul-thing or soul-substance is similarly conceived as a perfectly simple and absolutely self-identical somewhat, which persists unchanged throughout the flux of our mental experience. It is something to which these experiences are attached or referred—something which supports them, so to speak, in existence. Conceiving the soul thus as a changeless unit, the scholastic metaphysicians and their successors proceeded to argue from its unity and simplicity to its indiscerptibility or indestructibility, and to demonstrate, in short, its necessary immortality. If the essential characteristic of the soul is the simplicity of the hypothetical atom—atom being understood in the traditional sense of an ultimate and indivisible particle—then, clearly, it is proof against all the forces of destruction which dissolve other things into their elements. It cannot be decomposed, for it is not a *compositum*. The argument is, in a sense, purely verbal. It is but defining the soul as a unitary simple being, and the thing is done. But in point of fact the soul is neither one, nor simple, in the sense required; and, if it were, its existence, however endless, would be absolutely without value.

If we ask what was the origin of the belief and what were the motives which gave rise to it, there can be little doubt that the substantial soul represents a survival of the primitive animistic idea of a ghostly double which leaves the body at death and enables us to think of the life of the dead man as continued in some fashion after the dissolution of the bodily frame. It is also plain, I think, that it is the interest in a future life which causes philosophers, as well as other men, to cling so tenaciously to the idea of a separate soul-substance, conceived as independent of the fate of the body. Both these points are conceded by Dr. McDougall, the most recent champion of the doctrine. On the title-page he describes his book on *Body and Mind* as 'a History and a Defence of Animism'; and in the preface he states his belief that 'the future of religion is intimately bound up with the fate of Animism', and that, with its repudiation, 'the belief in any form of life after the death of the body will continue rapidly to decline among all civilized peoples'. His book has been written, he tells us, with a 'desire to see the world-old belief in a future life established on a scientific foundation'. The interest of the Scholastics in the substantial soul was similarly based, and the same holds true of Descartes and the long succession of thinkers who have defended the doctrine in modern times. But the essential faiths of mankind show a surprising power of surviving the dogmas on which they have been supposed to rest. We need not, therefore, be deterred by any fear of consequences from the frankest scrutiny of these soul-substances. If, as I propose to argue, we find them superfluous for the explanation of our conscious experience during the present life, we can have no inducement to regard them as essential for the continuance of that experience after death.

The futility of such a substance as the bearer or support of the conscious life during our earthly span was convincingly driven home by Locke in the chapter on 'Identity and Diversity' which he added to the second edition of his *Essay*.[1] It might naturally be imagined that personal

[1] *Essay*, Bk. II. 27.

identity depended on, and was ultimately guaranteed by, identity of the underlying soul-substance. This seemed, indeed, to be the express function of substance in the older metaphysics. But so far is this from being the case [Locke argues] that we might have a single immaterial substance supporting a series of distinct personal lives—as is, indeed, supposed to be the case in theories of transmigration or rebirth—and, on the other hand, 'we might have two thinking substances and only one person'.[1] Personal identity, he rightly urges, depends on what he calls 'consciousness', the consciousness which accompanies every present experience and which 'can be extended backwards to any past action or thought'. 'As far as any intelligent being can repeat the idea of any past action with the same consciousness it had of it at first, and with the same consciousness it has of any present action; so far it is the same personal self. For it is by the consciousness it has of its present thoughts and actions that it is self to itself now, and so will be the same self as far as the same consciousness can extend to actions past or to come.' Locke appeals to the doctrine of transmigration to clinch his argument: 'Let any one suppose that he has in himself an immaterial spirit, and that it is the same soul that was in Nestor or Thersites at the siege of Troy . . . but he now having no consciousness of any of the actions either of Nestor or Thersites, does or can he conceive himself the same person with either of them . . . or think [their actions]

[1] Cf. Kant's similar argument in a note to the Paralogism of Rational Psychology in the first edition of the *Critique of Pure Reason*. He takes the analogy of an elastic ball striking full upon a similar one and imparting to the second all its motion. 'Let us assume substances after the analogy of such bodies. We might conceive a whole series of them, the first of which imparted its state and the consciousness thereof to the second; this again its own state, along with that of the first, to the third, &c. In such a case the last substance would be conscious of all the states of the previously changed substances as its own, since those states were transferred to it along with the consciousness of them.'

his own, more than the actions of any other man that ever existed . . . though it were ever so true that the same spirit that informed Nestor's or Thersites's body were numerically the same that now informs his?' And, on the other hand, 'Had I the same consciousness that I saw the Ark and Noah's flood, as that I saw an overflowing of the Thames last winter, or as that I write now, I could no more doubt that I who write this now, that saw the Thames overflow last winter, and that viewed the flood at the general deluge, was the same self, place that self in what substance you please, than that I who write this am the same myself now whilst I write (whether I consist of all the same substance, material or immaterial, or no) that I was yesterday. . . . I being as much concerned and as justly accountable for any action . . . done a thousand years since, appropriated to me now by this self-consciousness, as I am for what I did the last moment.'

The argument is conclusive. The immaterial substance is left without any function whatever to discharge, and Locke might have dismissed the idea then and there as 'the ghost of a departed entity'. He did indeed indicate his feeling of its superfluity, 'it being not much more remote from our comprehension to conceive that God can, if he pleases, superadd to matter a faculty of thinking, than that he should superadd to it another substance with a faculty of thinking'; and he hazarded the suggestion that 'all the great ends of morality and religion are well enough secured, without philosophical proofs of the soul's immateriality.'[1] But he does not press the point, and he does not himself definitely abandon the conception whose uselessness he so triumphantly demonstrates.

This conception of substance as an inert substratum or support of attributes whose coherence it does nothing to explain—degenerating, as in Locke, into an unkown

[1] *Essay*, Bk. IV. 3. 6.

somewhat, impenetrably hidden behind the veil of its own qualities—was, however, ripe for revisal, in the case of material no less than of immaterial substance. A thing, in Lotze's memorable phrase, is what it does; we read its nature or essence in its appearances, in the way it behaves. Let us take the case of material substances first. We are prone to imagine that in every single thing we call real there is present, as its kernel, a grain of reality-stuff, as Lotze says, somehow 'communicating to the properties gathered about it the fixedness and consistency of a Thing'. This tendency of the imagination is crystallized in popular metaphysics; and Lotze's exposure of the futility and inherent perversity of such a mode of conception is one of the finest examples of his penetrative analysis.[1] Philosophy, as he often quaintly says, does not exist to teach us 'how being is made'; and it is quite unintelligible how a set of qualities could be made real by attaching them to a kernel of qualityless stuff. 'Real' is an adjective or predicate which we apply to anything that behaves in a certain way—that changes, for example, in a regular order, and remains identical with itself within certain limits. We *seem* to unite two ideas in the conception of a Thing—that of the content by which it is distinguished from other things and that of its reality. But these are not two actually separable elements of its being; the reality is simply the law according to which the changeable states of the thing are connected with one another—the formula, so to speak, in which its life-history or its modes of behaviour are resumed or summarized. And lest the word 'law'—which usually suggests a general formula applicable to many individual instances—should mislead us into supposing that we are still moving in the region of the general or the abstract, Lotze compares the essence of a thing to a melody. In a melody the successive sounds obey a law

[1] *Metaphysics*, Bk. I, c. 3 [English Translation, pp. 57–75].

of aesthetic consecutiveness, but this law is at the same time recognized as something perfectly individual: the law constitutes the melody in question. Similarly 'the real thing is nothing but the individual law of its behaviour'; 'the essence is not a dead point behind its activity, but identical with it'. In short, the idea of substance, unless it determines the coherence of the qualities or the succession of the states, is entirely otiose.[1]

If we apply the same line of criticism in the case of the soul, it is plain that its reality or 'substantiality'—if we are to continue to use that term—consists in the unity and continuity which actually characterize its life, that conscious self-identity which Locke so impressively described. 'The fact of the unity of consciousness', says Lotze, 'is *eo ipso* at once the fact of the existence of a substance.' 'So far as, and so long as, the soul knows itself as this identical subject, it is, and is named, simply for that reason, substance. But the attempt to find its capacity of thus knowing itself in the numerical unity of another underlying substance ("a hard and indissoluble atom") is not a process of reasoning which merely fails to reach an admissible aim—it has no aim at all. That which is not only conceived by others as unity in multiplicity, but knows and makes itself good as such, is, simply on that account, the truest and most indivisible unity there can be.'[2]

This is admirably put; yet so strong is the fascination of the underlying substance that, in other passages, Lotze seems to reinstate it in its old position. Thus, although he says here that 'the fact of the unity of consciousness is

[1] As Professor Laird points out, Locke's account of the 'real essence' of bodies from which, if we knew it, we could deduce 'whole sheaves' of properties, as we can from the definition and construction of a triangle, is on the track of a truer conception of substance and its function than his usual treatment of it as an unknown and indifferent substratum. (*Problems of the Self*, p. 318).

[2] *Metaphysics*, sections 243-4.

eo ipso at once the fact of the existence', he says elsewhere that the unity is 'our *sufficient ground* for conceiving an indivisible soul'.[1] In the corresponding chapter of his more popular work, the *Microcosmus* (Bk. II, ch. 1) he again speaks of 'inferring' from the existence of our consciousness 'the unity of a being conscious of itself'; and he describes this 'being' quite frankly as 'the one ego lying unchanged alike beneath its simultaneous variety and its temporal succession. Every retrospect of the past brings with it this image of the ego as the combining centre.' This 'element of peculiar nature . . . lies *at the base* of the world of sensations, emotions and volitions, and by its own unity binds them into the whole of a rounded-off development'.[2] Similarly he talks, in his *Metaphysics*, of 'the absolutely indivisible unity of *that which is to support* our inward life'.[3]

A characteristically drastic phrase from William James's *Principles of Psychology* may perhaps serve best to bring home to us Lotze's distinctive view of the soul. James is commenting on one use which the soul-substance is supposed to have—one function which it alone is supposed to be capable of discharging. 'The bald fact is,' he says, 'that when the brain acts, a thought occurs. The spiritualistic formulation says that the brain processes *knock the thought, so to speak, out of a Soul* which stands there to receive their influence.'[4] As a matter of fact, Lotze states the position almost in James's words. 'A physical event does not become a condition of the rise of a feeling until the sum of motions in which it consists *meets with a subject which in its own nature has the peculiar capacity of producing feeling from itself.*'[5] He emphasizes the incomparability of the mental processes with their physical conditions—the

[1] *Metaphysics*, section 241.
[2] *Microcosmus*, English translation, i. 144, 154–5. [3] Section 242.
[4] *Principles of Psychology*, i. 345. [5] *Metaphysics*, section 239.

inconceivable nature of the transition from a series of physical movements to the conscious experiences of sweetness, brightness, or sound. 'The chasm is never bridged over between the last state of the material elements within our reach and the first rise of the sensation.' We require, therefore, to assume 'a special ground of explanation for psychic life'. However indissolubly mental states are associated with material conditions, 'anything that we can conceive as an energy or efficacy of matter, instead of producing mental life from itself, only occasions its manifestation by stimulating to expression a differently constituted element'.[1]

Now the real point of Lotze's contention here—as comes out more clearly in the course of the argument in his *Metaphysics*—is that it is unintelligible to speak of material motions producing mental life 'from themselves': or, in a later phrase, 'as the consequence of nothing beside them'.[2] Material motions can from themselves produce only further motions. The genesis of feeling or consciousness means something superadded, an entirely new mode of existence; and for that reason Lotze calls for a special 'ground of explanation', a special subject in which the new experiences shall be housed or to which they shall be attached. What he is combating is thus, in his own words, 'the *generatio aequivoca* of everything rational from that which is devoid of reason'. But it is only a hopelessly out-of-date materialism that thinks of the brain producing thought as the liver produces bile or as a kettle produces steam. In a process of creative evolution, as I have already urged,[3] we can never explain or deduce the higher from the lower; each step in advance is wholly inexplicable, if viewed from the step below. The

[1] *Microcosmus*, i. 148–50.

[2] *Metaphysics*, section 252.

[3] p. 70 *supra*. For the general argument compare *The Idea of God*, Lecture V, 'The Lower and the Higher Naturalism', pp. 92–108.

advance is due to the immanent spirit of the whole, present at each stage of the evolution. As Lotze himself so well says of this particular case, the result can only be regarded as 'a new creation produced by the one encompassing Being from its own nature, as the supplement of its physical activity there and then operating'.[1] But how does the hypothesis of a substantial soul help the explanation? The invocation of the soul would seem to be, as James argues, only an emphatic statement of our belief that the relation of the organic to the conscious facts is grounded in the nature of things.[2]

The real attraction of the soul-substance for the imagination appears to be the satisfaction it yields to the ingrained materialism of our ordinary thinking, which craves for

[1] *Ibid.*, section 251.

[2] To understand Lotze's position, we must remember that his earlier physiological work was largely a campaign against the old Vitalism; his aim was to clarify physiological conceptions and methods by expelling the mythological entity, 'Vital Force', and exhibiting all bodily processes as the result of known physical and chemical forces. The campaign was successful, and Lotze was left with the body, on the one hand, as a mechanism conceived in purely physical terms, and, on the other hand, the phenomena of consciousness which are the primary data of experience. He found the crude materialistic philosophy which was rampant in Germany during the forties and fifties of last century treating the conscious life as the ephemeral product of purely material forces. Lotze's campaign was really directed in the last resort against this crude and aggressive materialism, and his negative criticism of Vitalism was intended to prepare the way for the final struggle by making the issue clear. His strategy was to surrender to mechanism the utmost it could possibly claim, and then to demonstrate the inexorable limits set to its pretensions. The more clearly the nature of a pure mechanism was realized, he felt, the more impossible must it appear that mechanical conditions could, *of themselves*, generate feeling and thought. And in this he was right. But, having resolved to treat the body as no more than a machine, Lotze felt himself constrained to locate the distinctive capacities of consciousness in another subject which interacts with the bodily mechanism. This conception came to him the more easily seeing that not only is it in harmony with the traditional philosophic dualism, but the idea of monadic centres of consciousness had been familiar in Germany, since Leibniz, as the foundation of an idealistic philosophy.

a punctual unit, some solid particle, one may really say, in which the physical movements may terminate, on which they may impinge, and in which they may produce their effects. So we have seen Lotze speaking of the 'series of motions' continuing 'till it meets with a subject'; and he illustrates the need for such a subject by the example of the composition of movements or forces in mechanics. Forces acting in different directions are said to be compounded, as in the parallelogram of forces; but the compounding depends, he points out, on the presence of a particle on which they can both act, and in which the effects of their joint action are fused.[1] Dr. McDougall adopts the illustration: 'Without a particle to act upon, the several forces could produce no accelerations; just so the brain processes could produce no sensations except *by acting upon the soul.*' And, applying this to the psychical fusion of the effects of simultaneous sensory stimuli, he says, 'These facts can only be rendered intelligible by assuming that both processes influence or act upon *some one thing or being; and since this is not a material thing, it must be an immaterial thing.*'[2] We may certainly *call* it immaterial, but the name will not alter its nature; for this manner of speaking obviously reduces the relation of mind and body to a problem in mechanics, and we are confronted at once by all the difficulties which have been so familiar to European philosophy since the middle of the seventeenth century, when this very problem of interaction broke up the Cartesian School.

[1] *Metaphysics*, section 242.
[2] *Body and Mind*, pp. 297–9.

LECTURE V

MIND AND BODY

(continued)

AT the close of the last lecture we were criticizing the essentially materialistic conception of the soul or mind as a punctual unit on which the mechanical forces of the body impinge, and I recalled the ineffectual attempts of Descartes to formulate a theory of interaction on these lines. The story of the break-up of the Cartesian School under the pressure of this problem, the rise of Occasionalism and its ultimate development into the parallelistic theories of Spinoza and Leibniz, is so well known that even a *résumé* would be superfluous here. The more so, because the most recent statements by psychologists and philosophers do little more than repeat the occasionalistic criticism of interaction and propound some variety of psycho-physical parallelism as a way of escape from the difficulties raised. The types of possible theory are, as a matter of fact, strictly limited. The older Materialism, whether of the eighteenth or nineteenth century, with its easy-going account of thought as a 'secretion' or a 'function' of the brain, may be dismissed in a word or two as based on an abuse of language which conceals the whole difficulty. The secretion of the liver is itself material—is simply one stage in the endless transformations of energy which we call the material world. And if we say with Carl Vogt that 'just as contraction is the function of the muscles, so, and in the same way, does the brain generate thoughts, movements or feelings', we similarly forget that contraction, as a function of the muscles, means only a particular state of the muscles themselves, a series of movements which we can observe and picture to ourselves as taking place in space. 'But if we describe the brain at work there is no need to mention consciousness at all, and in naming and describing conscious processes there is no need to mention the brain.'[1] The fundamental confusion of thought which crude Materialism involves is sufficiently exposed in Huxley's often-quoted statement: 'How it is that anything so remarkable as a state of consciousness comes about as the result of irritating nervous tissue, is just as unaccountable as the appearance of the Djin when Aladdin rubbed his lamp, or any other ultimate fact of nature.'[2]

But while in such a sentence we leave crude Materialism behind us, most people must feel the theory which Huxley offers us in its stead to be, in its practical consequences, indistinguishable from the Materialism discarded. The theory in question is the Epiphenomenalism, or (in Huxley's own phrase) the 'conscious automatism' so confidently pressed upon the world in the seventies of last century as the last word of science. Emphasizing, like the Occasionalists, the essential inconceivableness of the transition from the physical to the mental or *vice versa*, and yet holding, as we must, to their actual correlation, Huxley is led to extend the Cartesian doctrine of animal automatism so as to make it cover the whole course of man's conscious life. 'Consciousness', he said in 1874, 'would appear to be related to the mechanism of the body simply as a collateral product of its working, and to be as completely without any power of modifying that working as the steam-whistle which accompanies the work of a locomotive engine is without influence on its machinery. It seems to me that in men, as in brutes, there is no proof that any state of consciousness is the cause of change in

[1] Stout, *Manual of Psychology*, 1st ed., p. 49.
[2] *Elementary Physiology*, Lesson 8.

the motion of the matter of the organism. If these positions are well based, it follows that our mental conditions are simply the symbols in consciousness of changes which take place automatically in the organism. We are conscious automata.'[1] Consciousness, on this theory, is thus a completely inactive accompaniment, a mere spectator, so to speak, of a causal chain of bodily changes which go on by themselves, a by-product, thrown off, it would appear, without any expenditure of bodily energy, and itself giving rise to no effects. It has been compared to the shadow which runs alongside the pedestrian without in any way influencing his steps; or, again, to a kind of aura or phosphorescence playing, as it were, on the surface of the bodily movements. The subjective pleasure or pain which seems to prompt our actions has in reality no such efficacy. It is simply an index-finger to certain independently proceeding nerve movements. The presence or absence of consciousness in short makes no difference to a physical process which in Clifford's words 'gets along entirely by itself'.[2]

But in assigning to consciousness this entirely superfluous rôle, the theory overshoots itself; for if consciousness makes no difference to a creature, how, it may be pertinently asked, did it ever come to be evolved? This simple criticism from the biological point of view has been so effectively driven home by William James, Professor Ward, and others, not to mention Mr. Bradley's delightfully ironic paper on 'The Supposed Uselessness of the Soul',[3] that I do not propose to labour it here. It is, to my mind, fundamental and conclusive. But it is worth adding that the whole conception of consciousness as purely cognitive —the passive mirror of existing fact—is false to every teaching of psychology. Consciousness has its face con-

[1] Essay on 'Animal Automatism', published in 1874, reprinted in *Collected Essays*, vol. i.

[2] Essay on 'Body and Mind', in 1874. [3] *Mind*, N.S. iv. (April 1895).

sistently turned to the future: it is essentially an active striving towards some end. The sense of this activity is for each of us our most intimate experience.

For these reasons the parallelistic theory in its one-sided epiphenomenalistic form, with causation restricted to the physiological series, has been very generally abandoned in favour of a more carefully stated doctrine of psycho-physical parallelism, which attempts to hold the balance more fairly between the two concomitant factors. In this form, the theory professes to acknowledge the efficaciousness of consciousness. The maxim, of course, still holds good, 'No psychosis without neurosis': but a neurosis accompanied by psychosis is not the same, it is allowed, as a neurosis which has no such concomitant. We must not, therefore, take the neural facts by themselves and treat them as the only causes in operation. If we use the letter A to symbolize a particular neurosis and the Greek letter α to symbolize the accompanying psychosis, A and α are inseparable elements of a single fact $A\alpha$; and if we symbolize the next stage in the causal series as $B\beta$, we have no right to say that the result was due either to A alone, as epiphenomenalism says, or to α, as common sense might say, meaning by α some conscious desire or volition. The volition may be truly spoken of as a cause, but it cannot operate save in conjunction with the corresponding neurosis. If we are to think and talk correctly, we must say that it is the total fact $A\alpha$ which is the cause of the subsequent fact $B\beta$. Parallelism, understood in some such sense, has been, Professor Stout asserts, 'for the last fifty years the orthodox creed of physiologists and psychologists alike, and even now is more widely accepted than any other.' It is the theory which he himself advocated in the first edition of his *Manual*. But it is noteworthy that, in the latest edition, he speaks with a much more uncertain voice. He enlarges upon the utter vagueness of what we mean by parallelism or correspondence when we come to grips with the actual problem, and the impossibility, indeed, of finding any precise physiological counterpart to the most characteristic features of conscious experience. In the end, he refuses to decide between parallelism and interaction, though still himself inclined to accept the former, at least as a principle of method.

It is not necessary here to go into any elaborate criticism of this amended theory, which is what is usually understood by psycho-physical parallelism in a specific sense. To me, I confess, the idea of two concomitant but uncommunicating and completely independent causal series seems a forced and unnatural hypothesis. It is intelligible only as a revulsion from a crudely expressed interactionism. In that respect it may to a certain extent enlist our sympathy; but I think we must agree with Professor Ward that 'invariable concomitance and causal independence are incompatible positions'.[1] According to the ordinary canons of scientific method, invariable concomitance is just what makes us certain that the two facts in question must be causally interdependent. It is really 'quite inconceivable', as James says, 'that consciousness should have *nothing to do* with a business which it so faithfully attends'.[2] The theory, I will only add, seems to me to occupy a position of very unstable equilibrium and to be continually on the point of relapsing into epiphenomenalism. Nor do I see how this can be otherwise, so long as it maintains the self-contained and insulated character of the physical and the psychical series respectively, and treats the course of events in the former series as completely determined by 'physical and chemical conditions acting according to physical and chemical laws'.[3]

The truth is that all these theories—the traditional view

[1] *Naturalism and Agnosticism*, ii. 24.
[2] *Principles of Psychology*, i. 136. [3] Stout, *Manual*, 3rd ed., p. 80.

of interaction as well as the various forms of parallelism—are governed by a common presupposition. They are all more or less laboured and unnatural attempts to escape from the *impasse* which that presupposition creates. They start with the assumption, on which the Cartesian doctrine depends, that the ultimate and literal truth about the material world is the account which physics gives of it as a self-contained system of mechanically determined movement. This is what has been called 'the Mechanistic dogma', and it obviously leaves no room for teleological or purposive activity in any form. But theories which proceed on this assumption have strangely forgotten the fact of Life. Hence, when they are ultimately brought up against that inconvenient fact, they have no resource but to deny, as Descartes did, that animals really *are* alive, or, as the Epiphenomenalists still more consistently do, that any one is alive at all. Neither man nor beast ever *does* anything, although movements take place in their bodily frames like those of the dead men in the *Ancient Mariner*.

> They raised their limbs like lifeless tools—
> We were a ghastly crew.
> The body of my brother's son
> Stood by me, knee to knee:
> The body and I pulled at one rope,
> But he said naught to me.

But such extravagant conclusions simply indicate the straits to which a theory may reduce us. It is in the end a stupidity to affect to ignore the fundamental difference between a living being and any collection of what we call dead matter. And it is equally useless to try to minimize the difference, however easy it may be, here as in similar instances, to point to marginal cases, transitional forms, whose status is perhaps open to doubt. There is no broader contrast imprinted on the face of nature, as primitive man was quick to recognize.

The relevant facts in which the difference consists may

be simply enough stated. In the first place, an organism, although its parts are outside of one another in space, is a unity or whole in a sense in which that cannot be asserted of any inorganic thing. It seems actively to constitute itself a separate whole. It is a natural unity, *unum per se*, in Leibniz's phrase,[1] as against the *unum per accidens* of inorganic things, which is a unity more or less arbitrarily carved out of nature's continuum according to human interests and purposes. An organism asserts itself against its environment as such a natural unity: it *acts* as a whole. Its actions are selective in the interest of the whole, self-preservative, self-recuperative. The fundamental assumption of biology is that of a creature thus maintaining and reproducing its structure and activities as a whole, in the face of varying environment. Terms like stimulus, response, behaviour, all imply the notion of selection, the power of adaptation to environmental change, by which the organism maintains and develops its own characteristic being. Physics knows no such self-maintaining individuals—only a continuous transmutation of energy; and the physicist is therefore tempted to swamp the organism, as it were, in its environment—to treat the living being simply as a network of pathways through which the energy of external nature takes its course. But such a conception does not fit the facts even in the case of the humblest organism. As Professor Ward says, 'The more the protoplasmic movements, even of the lowest plants, are studied, the more they are found to resemble actions determined by stimuli and to deviate from the mechanical motions of inert masses.'[2]

It was the appreciation of this characteristic difference between the living and the non-living that led an older generation of physiologists to the theory of a 'vital force',

[1] *Philosophische Schriften* (Gerhardt), iii. 657.
[2] *Naturalism and Agnosticism*, i. 285.

present in the organism, directing the mechanical agencies at work, and so accounting for the purposive character of the resultant movements. But 'vital force' is obviously what Comte would call a metaphysical entity of the most approved pattern, being simply the phenomenon itself in duplicate, hypostatized as its own cause. It repeats more-over the worst faults of the soul-substance, being conceived as an additional force of the physical order introduced into the bodily complex and operating mechanically upon those already at work. Hence the more clear-sighted physiolo-gists started a vigorous campaign against this unverifiable entity, the invocation of which they regarded, not unjustly, as a form of *ignava ratio*, paralysing research into the real causation of physiological facts. The scientific ideal, they contended, ought to be to exhibit all bodily processes as the result of known physical and chemical forces. This campaign, carried out in the first half of last century, drove vitalism from the field; and during the remainder of the century physiological science continued to pursue this mechanistic ideal, which, it may be freely admitted, proved itself eminently successful as a methodological precept in detailed research. Hence the rule of method speedily passed into a dogma, while the larger considerations which had prompted the vitalist hypothesis were simply left on one side. But they were bound to reassert them-selves on fuller reflection. As philosophy and science drew nearer to one another in the closing years of the century, the sufficiency of the mechanistic explanation was once more challenged among trained physiologists by a number of active thinkers who did not hesitate to say that, instead of coming nearer, the reduction of biological processes to terms of mechanism appeared to recede, as knowledge became deeper and more intimate, and that, in short, no vital process whatever, however simple and, at first sight, purely physical it might seem, admitted of adequate statement in merely physical terms. This 'neo-vitalism' is not exempt, I think, from a tendency to err, as the old vitalism erred. It seems, in some of its statements, to vest the central control of the nervous processes in a separate entity, which, by some kind of interference *ab extra*, modifies and directs a course of events which is otherwise conceived as proceeding on purely mechanical principles. But this is to miss everything that is of value in the new conception of the organism. The whole point of the view for which I have contended is that nothing happens inorganically in a living creature at all—except, of course, when what we call an accident happens to it; and even then, if the damage has not gone too far, the organism at once sets about growing new tissue to repair the mischief. If we are wise, we shall not seek to explain *how* the organism comes to behave as it does. Life is an ultimate fact, whose nature, like that of other ultimate facts, has, in a sense, just to be accepted. If we try to get behind it—to see the 'works', as we might say—we can only end by breaking it up into parts which we cannot put together again. The real task of the man of science or the philosopher is not such pseudo-explanation, but simply accurate description.

If we realize, then, the fact of life and its nature, we escape at once from the hopeless dualism between pure spirit on the one side and a dead world of physical forces on the other. The living body is the concrete reality with which we have to deal, and we recognize that the scheme of mass-points and forces to which the physicist reduces the world, so far from representing the ultimate reality of things, is no more than an abstract construction for his own immediate purposes. Some one has wittily remarked that the customary conception of man treats the human being as 'a mechanical union of a corpse and a ghost'. This is, at any rate, no inapt description of the

Cartesian theory or of the Epiphenomenalism in whic
the corpse drags the pithless ghost unresistingly in it
train. But the living being bridges the imaginary gul
Pure spirit, so far as our experience goes, is an abstrac
tion. If we start with the living body as the embodie
soul, the problem of interaction ceases to exist an
laboured schemes of parallelism become unnecessary.

A point not less important—for our purpose, indeed
specially important—is, that if we start thus with a
adequate conception of the organism, we shall be o
the way to a better understanding of the kind of unit
which can really belong to soul or self. I have alread
referred to the stress laid by philosophers on the unit
of the soul and the argument for immortality which the
base upon that unity. And we saw how Plato contraste
the unity and simplicity of the soul with the multiple
and composite character of the body. Many philosopher
have followed him in emphasizing the same contrast. I
is very common, for example, to point out that the brain
extended as it is in space, and consisting of many parts
furnishes no analogue to the unity of consciousness, an
consequently offers no foundation for it. Even if w
suppose the various items of our experience—the objectiv
data furnished by the senses—to be correlated with th
functioning of different parts of the brain, we canno
suppose the unitary act in which they are apprehende
to be, as one writer puts it, 'distributed over an aggregat
of separate atoms'.[1] 'The unity of consciousness', say
the same writer, 'is incompatible with a multiplicity o
elements of whatever kind.' Therefore, to explain th
unity of any act of thought, we are forced, the argumen
concludes, to assume an ego or soul—that is to say, a
indivisible immaterial being—as the real subject of ou

[1] Maher, *Psychology*, p. 467.

experience. But such a line of argument ignores the fact that, although the parts of an organism, if we regard it physically, are certainly external to one another, it is the very nature of an organism, if regarded functionally (that is to say, *as* an organism), to transcend this mutual exclusiveness. The parts of an organism are so much members one of another and of the whole which they constitute—they are so interpenetrative in their action—that it is hardly a paradox to say that the organism *qua* organism is not in space at all. Part and whole acquire here a meaning unknown to physics, a meaning in which the necessary correlation of the terms is for the first time apparent.[1] The organism, as we have already seen, is the first real whole, the first natural unity. It exhibits a unity in multiplicity far more impressive and far more important than the punctual unity of the hypothetical atom. And it has often been pointed out that in this unity and mutual implication of whole and parts we have the best analogue of the *kind* of unity which we may expect to find, still more intimately realized, in the self-conscious being. Unfortunately, philosophers have too generally found their exemplar in the solid singleness of the atom or the abstract identity of the mathematical point.

We have already traced the influence of this false ideal in the doctrine of the soul-substance. But even in quarters where the soul-substance is disavowed, or at least held in the background, the idea of an unchanging unit still persists. Thus we found Lotze, after his incisive criticism of the soul-substance, still speaking of 'the one Ego lying unchanged alike beneath the simultaneous variety and the temporal succession' of our conscious states.[2] The following statement by Reid may be taken

[1] I may perhaps refer to an early essay of my own on 'Philosophy as Criticism of Categories', in which this argument is elaborated. The paper is reprinted in *The Philosophic Radicals and other Essays.*

[2] Cf. p. 79 *supra.*

as typical. 'My personal identity implies the continued existence of that indivisible thing which I call myself. . . . My thoughts, and actions, and feelings, change every moment—they have no continued, but a successive existence; but that *Self* or *I*, to which they belong, is permanent, and has the same relation to all the succeeding thoughts, actions, and feelings, which I call mine.'[1] This 'indivisible thing', standing in relation to all the contents of consciousness, but not itself woven, so to speak, of the same stuff, not itself an element in the process, reappears in many more recent arguments. The Animist, says Dr. McDougall, 'maintains that the consciousness of any individual is or has a unity of a unique kind and that it cannot properly be regarded as consisting of elements, units or atoms of consciousness put together or compounded in any way. He maintains . . . that we are logically bound to infer *some ground of this unity other than consciousness itself.*'[2] Dr. McDougall goes on to claim Lotze as 'the greatest modern defender of Animism'. I do not think that Lotze would have subscribed to all Dr. McDougall's statements of what he takes to be their common position; but his fundamental argument for the unity of consciousness—that the simplest comparison of two ideas, and the recognition of them as like or unlike, presupposes 'the indivisible unity of that which compares them'—certainly suggests the same idea of the subject as external to the content with which it deals. 'It must be one and the same thing (Lotze adds) which first forms the idea of *a*, then that of *b*, and which at the same time is conscious of the nature and extent of the difference between them.'[3] This is uncomfortably like Reid, and we cannot forget that, in the passages previously quoted,[4] Lotze repeatedly referred to this identical subject as that which 'supports' or 'lies at

[1] *Intellectual Powers*, Essay III, c. 4.
[2] *Body and Mind*, pp. 282–3.
[3] *Metaphysics*, section 241.
[4] p. 79, *supra*.

he base of' our inward life. These and other phrases all seem to imply that the unity is not the conscious unity reached *in* the experience, but 'an element of peculiar nature' (as he calls it) existing somehow outside of the process, a Subject whose the experiences are, set as a static unity over against the flux of psychical content, and remaining identical with itself through all the changes of that content.

Similar expressions in regard to the unity of consciousness occur in Kant and in Green, and they are perhaps difficult to avoid. But in Kant and in Green—in Kant at any rate—they are put forward in the course of a logical inquiry into the conditions of knowledge. The 'I think', the unity of apperception which Kant 'deduces' as the supreme condition of the possibility of experience, is expressly stated by him to be the 'logically simple subject' which is 'the form of every judgement as such', or again, 'the possibility of the logical form of all knowledge'. This 'merely logical qualitative unity of self-consciousness in thinking'—this unity of the Self which for Kant is indistinguishable from the unity of the object, from 'the necessary connexion which we mean by the word nature' —has nothing to do, he insists, with the substantiality or simplicity of the individual thinking subject. To suppose that it has, is just the paralogism of the old rational psychology—the argument from the unity of the soul to its indestructibility—which he conclusively exposed. And he repeatedly tells us that this 'single self-consciousness', 'this I or he or it which thinks is in itself a perfectly empty and contentless idea', 'a transcendental Subject which we may represent as x', no more than 'the form of experience in general'. It is not necessary to subscribe to any of Kant's specific doctrines to recognize the truth on which he insists in such passages—that, when we isolate the subject as a purely formal activity or function of thought, and set it, so to speak, over against all its specific experiences, it becomes completely empty or contentless. It is the abstract idea of function or activity in general, and there is nothing in it to distinguish one individual self from another. It is almost unmeaning to talk of such a self as continuing to exist and maintaining its self-identity through the succession of its experiences, because it has no quality by which it is recognizable apart from its experiences, no existence except in those experiences. So conceived, it is not to be looked on as a concrete reality at all; as Kant says, it is a logical abstraction.

Hume's famous analysis of the Self contains, indeed, far more truth than is commonly conceded to it. It has suffered from the paradoxical form in which it is presented, and because it is put forward in the context of a purely sceptical theory. But Hume's criticism of a self which is distinct from all its states and which remains the same through all their changes is, in point of fact, unanswerable; and his celebrated description of the mind as 'nothing but a bundle or collection of different perceptions, which succeed each other with an inconceivable rapidity, and are in a perpetual flux and movement'[1] is defective only because of the psychological atomism on which his whole theory is based. By his psychological atomism I mean the twin principles which Hume himself signalizes[2] as the axiomatic presuppositions of his thinking, 'that all our distinct perceptions are distinct existences' and 'that the mind never perceives any real connexion among distinct existences'. Proceeding on these assumptions, Hume falls into the opposite error to that which he attacks; he ends by substantiating particular 'perceptions' as independently existing facts without any principle of organic connexion

[1] *Treatise*, Bk. I. 4. 6.

[2] In the Appendix to the third volume of the *Treatise*, in 1740.

between them: and the mind appears consequently as a casual 'collection' or 'bundle' of associated items. The defect is of course fatal; mere succession is no more adequate as an account of the mind than abstract identity. But that need not blind us to the relative truth of Hume's statement, 'they are the successive perceptions only that constitute the mind', if we take that statement simply as a negative criticism of the traditional doctrine of the simple identical self.

The same relative truth is expressed, also in a paradoxical and challenging form, in William James's dictum that 'the passing thought is the only thinker'. Or, to be more accurate, James, in this statement, seeks to give us the truth of Hume's contention, relieved of the psychological atomism which invalidates it in Hume and in the Associationists who followed him. James sees clearly that, if we start with detached feelings, expressly defined as 'distinct existences' with no 'real connexion' observable between them—or, as he expresses it himself, 'simple feelings, non-cognitive, non-transcendent of themselves, "ideas", each separate, each ignorant of its mate'[1]—it is pure mythology to imagine them 'gumming themselves together on their own account'.[2] Two similar ideas cannot yield an idea of similarity, nor two successive ideas an idea of succession, except to a knower who transcends and in some way includes the separate items. 'One must *beg* memory', he says.[3] That 'later feelings are aware of those that went before is no "theory" of the phenomena,' he contends, 'but a simple statement of them'.[4] 'The present passing thought' is, therefore, in James's account, the 'psychic integer' from which we start; it is to be taken, however, not as a self-contained unit knowing only itself, but, as we really find it in life, appropriating to

[1] *Principles of Psychology*, i. 359.
[2] *Ibid.*, 338.
[3] *Ibid.*, 389.
[4] *Ibid.*, 359 *n.*

itself all the thoughts or states that went before. This present thought or state, which James calls the judging Thought (with a capital T) is thus the final heir and owner of all its predecessors. It knows them and appropriates their content to itself. It is, as James puts it, 'the hook from which the chain of past selves dangles, planted firmly in the Present. . . . Anon the hook itself will drop into the past with all it carries, and then be treated as an object and appropriated by a new Thought in the new present, which will serve as living hook in turn.'[1] The appropriation of past states of mind depends, he goes on to say, on the feeling of warmth and intimacy which accompanies them. That 'animal warmth', as he frequently calls it, depending as it doubtless does to a large extent on the vague mass of organic feeling which is the continuous background of our more explicit consciousness, is the pronounced characteristic of any present conscious experience; and it is some degree of the same warmth which causes us to appropriate past experiences as ours. If we add to this the feeling of continuity between such past experiences and the present—a continuity realized, of course, not without gaps, but clearly enough marked through certain remembered stretches of time, and most vividly, as is natural, in the way our most recent experiences melt by slow degrees into the Self of the present moment—we have, in these two elements of resemblance and continuity, the fundamental factors in our sense of personal identity.

James states his points, as usual, in a series of vivid metaphors; but this conception of the present consciousness as the inheritor of all its past, the 'final receptacle', as he says, and at the same time the living point of further growth—as itself, so long as it exists, the actual self—seems

[1] *Principles of Psychology*, i. 340–1.

to me an infinitely truer way of representing the march of our conscious life than the conventional idea of an unchanging self or Ego outside of the succession altogether, and supposed, by its 'relating activity', to bring connexion and unity into a series of otherwise unrelated and disconnected items. The self must be constituted by its experiences; there is no other stuff of which it can be woven. As Hume rightly saw, it does *not* possess the perfect simplicity and identity of an atomic unit; it is a very complex structure. Hume's error lay in denying that there was any real unity or connexion in the structure at all. The words he uses to describe it are an explicit denial of such attributes. A 'bundle' or 'collection', he says in his most famous passage; 'a heap or a collection' in another place:[1] all terms which imply a mere aggregate of separate items which just happen to be swept together into that particular heap or collection. But in the course of the section on 'Personal Identity' he does alight once or twice upon a more adequate phrase, as when he says: 'The true idea of the human mind is to consider it as a system of different perceptions or different existences, which are linked together by the relation of cause and effect';[2] or again, in the same context: 'I cannot compare the soul more properly to anything than to a republic or commonwealth, in which the several members are united by the reciprocal ties of government and subordination, and give rise to other persons, who propagate the same republic in the incessant changes of its parts.' The second metaphor is somewhat vague, but the idea of system or of the unity in multiplicity which characterizes a state or an organism supplies just what was lacking in his original account of the soul. Do we need a soul in any other sense—or can we understand what is meant by

[1] *Treatise*, Bk. I. 4. 2 (Green and Grose, i. 495).
[2] *Treatise*, Bk. I. 4. 6 (Green and Grose, i. 541–2).

a soul in any other sense—than the systematic unity of the conscious experiences of a particular individual centre—the individual centre being defined or determined at the outset by the bodily organism?

That the mind or self does exist as such a system—a system of memories and associations, of preferences and dislikes, desires and purposes—is a fact of which we have each of us direct experience every day of our lives. Introspection, it is true, does not reveal to us at any given moment the whole system, but it discloses the general structure and such particular elements as are connected with the present interests which prompt our review; and we know that, with other promptings, we might continue the process of exploration indefinitely in other directions. We know, in short, to put it crudely, *the kind of thing the self is*, the nature of the existence which it enjoys, and the kind of unity and continuity which it actually possesses. This coherent unity of experience *is* the self, mind, or soul, in the only intelligible sense of these words; and no fact can be better attested than the actuality of such selves, minds, or souls. It is important to bear this in mind; for if, as we have been arguing, it is wrong to think of the self as a unitary something apart from and over against its states or experiences, it is no less illegitimate to think of the states as so many detached and evanescent facts. This, as we saw, was the error in Hume's account, and it is a mistake into which we are constantly apt to fall when we are thinking of the relation of body and mind. James's statement, quoted in the preceding lecture, 'the bald fact is just that when the brain acts a thought occurs'—true enough as a bit of polemic against the soul-substance—is perhaps open to criticism as suggesting that the relation between the bodily and the mental is to be understood simply as point-to-point correspondence of a passing thought with a passing brain-state. So conceiving the matter, we easily lapse into thinking of the brain as the enduring reality, and the successive conscious states as sparks struck by the working of the machine, a series of flashes which break upon the eye and pass away. And that of course is pure materialism. It is the natural result of treating conscious states as if they existed independently in a kind of objective fashion. Modern psychology has sometimes boasted of being a psychology without a soul, intending by that, mainly, the repudiation of the soul-substance; but no psychology can dispense with the conception of a subject. We must recognize, as Stout puts it, that 'there is a mind and not merely mental states or processes'.[1] The would-be neutral term 'states of consciousness' is an unsuccessful attempt to evade the acknowledgement that every conscious or mental state is the state or experience of a conscious individual. 'The universal conscious fact is not "feelings and thoughts exist", but "I think" and "I feel".'[2]

So understood, the unity of the subject is germinally present in the simplest sensation: what we have is not a feeling, but a self feeling in a certain way. The self is doubtless definable at the outset only in terms of its primitive sense-experiences; it is not to be regarded as anything substantially distinct from them. And similarly, the complex self of later life, the self of so many memories and interests and hopes—which is so much more, therefore, than any passing experience—owes its complexity, its whole structure and character, to the consolidated experience of which it is the organized unity. But we cannot describe mental facts at all without assuming an individual subject in this sense; they take from the beginning this personal form. From the beginning, consequently, each experience

[1] *Manual*, p. 18.

[2] James, *Principles of Psychology*, i. 226 (quoted from B. P. Bowne, and endorsed by James).

is an element in a growing self-integrating whole. The conditions which determine the individual unity of such a whole—the closed nature of the individual self, which prevents the experiences of Paul from straying into Peter's mind, like cattle into a neighbour's compound—are obviously of an organic nature. Every soul known to us is an embodied soul: it is the bodily conditions which, in the Tennysonian phrase, 'strike its being into bounds'. The body is, in this sense, the medium through which the soul comes into existence, so that we might almost speak, I said, of the body growing a soul, although acknowledging in the same breath that the genesis of consciousness in connexion with organic processes is something which it is ridiculous to suppose we could ever understand, in the sense of explaining it from the organic conditions themselves. The nature of conscious experience is simple and ultimate; it can be understood from within, but it cannot be mechanically put together.

Neither the original emergence of a rudimentary feeling subject nor the consolidation of subsequent experiences into the systematic unity of the mature self is really explained, I must repeat, or made in any way more easy of comprehension (except for the imagination), by locating the successive thoughts or feelings in the empty focus of an immaterial substance or an unchanging ego. Dr. McDougall, the latest champion of the animistic soul, lays great stress on 'the numerical distinctness of streams of consciousness' and 'the individual unity of the separate streams' to which I have just alluded. He says, very truly, that 'the hanging together of a multiplicity of conscious processes in a numerically distinct or individual stream is the very essence of soul or spirit', and constitutes 'a fundamental fact with which every psychological theory and every metaphysical system must deal'. Without this unity and coherence, he says, 'there would be nothing that could be called spirit or mind, but rather a mere chaos of mind-stuff'; and the problem over which he puzzles himself, and with which he seeks to closure his opponents, is 'What holds consciousness together?'[1] The soul is the causal agent which he invokes to effect the desired result. But surely this is an instance of the fruitless and essentially absurd desire to know 'how being is made'. The unity and coherence of the conscious experience is, as he himself says, 'the very essence of soul or spirit'; that is to say, it is what we mean by the words. It constitutes the existence of a soul. To seek to explain that real fact by saying that it is due to the presence and agency of a soul is, therefore, simply to restate the characteristic nature of the fact, and hypostatize it as a causal *prius* of its own existence. What explanation can we conceivably hope to give of a fact like the ultimate nature of consciousness? Are we really to think of the constituent items flying loose and of a soul or spirit as some kind of apparatus which supervenes to grip and hold them together? Surely Paulsen's attitude, which Dr. McDougall condemns and is inclined to deride, is the only reasonable one. 'It is a fact', Paulsen says, 'that the processes of the inner life do not occur in isolation, and that each is lived with the consciousness of belonging to the unitary whole of this undivided life. How this can happen I do not pretend to say, any more than I can say how consciousness itself is possible.'[2]

Let us, then, finally dismiss this idea of the substantial soul as some sort of supernatural mechanism to hold the conscious experiences together, and if we must indulge our imagination with the picture of some bearer of the

[1] *Body and Mind*, pp. 163-4. The phrase was struck out in conversation with Professor Strong, and in its exact formulation was apparently due to the latter, but it is evidently adopted by Dr. McDougall as an apt and trenchant expression of the difficulty.

[2] *Einleitung in die Philosophie*, p. 386, quoted by McDougall, p. 164.

conscious life, let us be satisfied with the body, in which that life is certainly rooted in a very real sense. For, although we no longer identify ourselves with the body, it remains for each of us, throughout life, the centre from which we speak and act and look out upon the universe. Not even the most abstract philosopher can escape from this pictorial way of thinking. But common sense does not feel that, in yielding to this natural tendency, it is committing itself to any banal materialistic view of consciousness as no more than a function or attribute of the body. The ordinary man feels instinctively that such a view precisely inverts the true proportion between the bodily facts and the conscious life. In this inner life he is aware of a coherent selfhood, constituted by memories of all that he has done and suffered, of the friends he has known and loved, the causes for which he has fought, as well as memories—intensest of all in their personal significance—of wrong done, of bitter remorse or repentance unto life, and, together with all these memories, his manifold present interests, his plans and purposes for himself or for others, and the ultimate aspirations which are the spirit of his life. This conscious self, shaped by all its experiences, and resuming them in an intense and characteristic unity, he feels to possess a reality to which the facts of the animal life on which it is reared appear merely accessory: he is ready to agree with Socrates and Plato that *this* is his 'true self', not the body which he carries about with him. It is this conviction, in fact, which inspires the persistent assertion of the self-subsistent reality of the soul or spirit, and which has led philosophers to call it a substance—substance being in its original intention, as has been well said, 'a descriptive term indicating a unity which exists *de facto*'.[1] But, as we have seen, the malicious sprite which presides over the destiny of philosophical terms unfortunately contrived that this well-meant affirmation came

[1] Professor Laird's *Study in Realism*, p. 172.

to imply the assimilation of the spiritual fact to a material thing. Let us stand by what is true in the assertion, but eschew a terminology so full of unfortunate associations.

A man's self will then be for us the coherent mind and character which is the result of the discipline of time, not some substantial unit or identical subject present in his body all along. We shall hold that, where such an evolution has been achieved, the self-conscious life is the pre-eminent reality which the body in its structure and organization exists to actualize. As a result of the evolution, the centre of gravity has been, as it were, completely shifted. The man, the concrete individual, can be adequately or properly described only in terms of personality or character—by reference to his dispositions and affections, his interests and ideals. Beside these, the bodily facts, as such, sink into insignificance, dear and familiar as they are as elements in the whole. And instead of being an intermittent and evanescent accompaniment of organic processes, the spiritual self, created through the bodily medium, is seen to achieve a unity and identity more complete and more permanent than can belong to any non-self-conscious being. It is, indeed, only the self-conscious spirit—a being who can make himself his own object and contemplate himself as a self—that attains individuality and independence in an ultimate sense. Every other being is, as it were, a channel of the Universal Will; but man, as self-conscious, can distinguish himself even from his Maker, and set his own will against the divine. Is it, then, unreasonable to conclude that an individuality so real, and the goal apparently of an age-long process, must be capable of surviving the dissolution of the material frame through which it was brought into being? The body, ceasing to be a living body, may relapse into its elements when it has 'fulfilled' itself, while the true individual, in which that fulfilment consisted, pursues his destiny under new conditions.

LECTURE VI

REINCARNATION AND KARMA

THE analysis of the nature of the spiritual self in the last two lectures has provided us with certain principles of judgement by which theories of immortality or of a future life must be tested. One of the oldest forms in which the belief in an after-life has been held, and, if we take the whole human race into consideration, still perhaps the form most widely persistent, is that of reincarnation or the transmigration of souls. The idea of a reincarnation of the souls of the dead arises at a primitive level from simple enough considerations. Family resemblances suggest that a child has inherited the soul of some deceased ancestor. There is also nothing unnatural, at such a level of thought, in supposing human souls to migrate into the bodies of beasts. Man, the nomad and the hunter, is a keen observer of animal ways and idiosyncracies. And here again resemblance probably suggested the idea. 'The half-human features and actions and character of animals', says Tylor,[1] 'are watched with wondering sympathy by the savage, as by the child. The beast is the very incarnation of familiar qualities of man; and such names as lion, bear, fox, owl, parrot, viper, worm, when we use them as epithets, condense into a word some leading feature of a human life.' Nor, in this connexion, must we forget the strange system of totemistic thought which explains so much in primitive religion and primitive society. The blood-brotherhood of the primitive wandering clan has, as its complement—its

[1] *Primitive Culture*, ii. 15.

religious sanction and seal—a similar blood-brotherhood with some bird or beast, conceived as the mythical ancestor of the clan and in some sense as its protective providence —to all intents and purposes, indeed, the clan-god. At death every member of the clan is supposed to rejoin his totem, and to assume the shape, therefore, of the animal in question. With the decay of totemism the obligation to rejoin the totem-animal disappears, but it remains easy to conceive the soul of a dead man passing into *some* kind of animal; and in this looser form the idea is found persisting among savage tribes alongside of the more general belief in an individual survival of a shadowy kind in some spirit-land.

Transmigration into some animal shape formed part of the doctrine of reincarnation on its first appearance in Europe in a religious setting in the Orphic and Pythagorean tradition. 'What is the opinion of Pythagoras concerning wild fowl?' So the clown catechizes Malvolio, and the unhappy gentleman's answer comes pat, 'That the soul of our grandam might haply inhabit a bird.' To Xenophanes, almost a contemporary, we owe the story of Pythagoras remonstrating with a man who was beating a dog, because in the howling of the animal he recognized the voice of a departed friend. If the spice of malice in the anecdote inclines us to regard it as *ben trovato* rather than literally true, it is at least unimpeachable evidence of the nature of Pythagoras's teaching. Empedocles also, who belonged to the neighbouring island of Sicily, and who reproduces in his poem many tenets of the Pythagorean brotherhood, professed, like the Master, to remember a number of his previous incarnations: 'Before this I was born once a boy, and a maiden, and a plant, and a bird, and a darting fish in the sea.' For primitive thought such transmigrations have no ethical significance, but in the Pythagorean and Orphic doctrine, as we have seen, the idea of retribution is prominent. In the cycle of births the soul expiates the primal sin by which it fell from its first estate and came to be imprisoned in a material body; and the particular kind of creature into which it passes in successive lives is also determined, as we saw in Plato's myths, by the kind of life led in the previous incarnation. In the East, as is well known, the doctrine of reincarnation became the basis of the most elaborate scheme of moral retribution ever offered to the world in the name of religion. But in so far as Brahmanism has incorporated in its system the idea of the transmigration of human souls into the bodies of lower animals, it has simply taken over the primitive animistic idea of the soul; and this part of the system we must hold to be definitely ruled out by the line of thought we have followed in the last two lectures. Transmigration in this sense is an idea impossible to any one who has realized the organic relation which undoubtedly exists between the *kind* of body and the *kind* of soul. The general idea of reincarnation calls, however, for some further examination, both in itself and on account of the doctrine of Karma with which it is inseparably bound up in Eastern thought.

The doctrine of Karma does not appear in the old Vedic hymns. At that early stage there is nothing of the pessimism which afterwards invaded Indian thought. The Vedic religion is in the main a simple worship of the powers of nature. 'Life is thought of as a blessing, and men pray that they may survive a hundred lengthened autumns.'[1] When death comes, they pass by 'the way of the Fathers' to the paradise ruled over by Yama, the first man to die, a world of light where all longings are fulfilled. That at least is the destiny of the brave and good; for the bad there waits a prison of fathomless darkness, and the later texts develop the horrors of hell

[1] Sidney Cave, *Living Religions of the East*, p. 21.

in the most copious and lurid fashion. The doctrine of reincarnation and Karma is first introduced in the Upanishads, about 600 B.C., as the great secret which solves the problem of human destiny. Karma means 'work' or 'deed', and the word is used to express an inexorable law of moral causation, represented as fulfilling itself in the life-history of each individual agent.

> The evil that men do lives after them;
> The good is oft interred with their bones,

says Shakespeare, but according to the doctrine of Karma, good and evil actions alike bear their fruit, and the fruit is all garnered by the individual agent himself. In the strictest and minutest sense, whatsoever a man soweth that shall he also reap. Man is thus continually shaping his own destiny. Every evil deed must be expiated—the penalty paid to the uttermost farthing—while every good deed will receive its appropriate reward. But the scene of expiation or reward is not another world—a hell or heaven in which the same self-conscious individual continues to exist with a memory of the past whose consequences he is reaping: the consequences of a man's actions are reaped by the agent on earth in a fresh incarnation.[1] Hence the saying 'A man is born into the world he has made.' According to another saying, 'As amongst a thousand

[1] As a matter of fact, however, the older belief in heaven and hell (or rather in multitudinous heavens and hells) is inconsistently retained and combined with the new doctrines in the fashion with which we are already familiar in Plato's myths, long periods being assumed between the successive incarnations, in the course of which the souls have already received the rewards or punishments due for their previous life. But, in spite of this fundamental inconsistency, the doctrine of reincarnation is the characteristic feature of the Eastern theory, as compared with doctrines of future retribution to which we are accustomed in the West. Plato, it may be noted, not only embodies the inconsistency in his own myths, but expressly mentions the duplication of punishment as 'a tradition which is firmly believed by many, and has been received from those who are learned in the mysteries' (*Laws*, 870).

cows a calf knows its mother, so the deed done beforetime finds out its doer.'[1] Requital, that is to say, is in every case personal. This doctrine of Karma and reincarnation became from henceforth, it has been well said, 'the logical *prius* of all Indian thought'.[2] It is the basal presupposition of Buddhism quite as much as of the Brahmanism from which Buddha revolted.

The theory of Karma, although its bearing upon the future is obvious, is thus primarily an explanation of a man's lot in the present life as determined by his own actions in a series of previous lives. As Professor Rhys Davids says, 'it is this pre-existence aspect of the theory which plays the greatest part and has the greatest vitality both in the older teaching and in modern Buddhism. The doctrine of Karma was never intended to be so much an explanation of what would happen to men after death as an explanation, drawn from the past, of what was now happening to him during life.'[3] If it is true that whatsoever a man soweth, that shall he also reap, the believer in Karma holds it must be equally true that whatsoever a man reaps, that he must also have sown. His personal qualities, his health and sickness, his caste and rank, his wealth or poverty—all the circumstances of his lot—are accounted for in this way. In the Brahmanic and Buddhistic systems this is worked out with the most painstaking minuteness. For every shade of guilt there is a fitting punishment, exactly adjusted to the offence in severity and duration. 'The stealer of food shall be dyspeptic, the scandalmonger shall have foul breath, the horse-stealer shall go lame, stealers of grain and meats shall turn into rats and vultures, the thief who took dyed garments or perfumes shall become a red partridge or a musk-rat.'[4]

[1] Professor A. G. Hogg, *Karma and Redemption*, p. 16.
[2] Cave, *op. cit.*, p. 31.
[3] *Hibbert Lectures*, p. 115.
[4] Tylor, *Primitive Culture*, ii. 8.

Again, 'a child may be born blind. This is owing to his lust of the eye in a previous life. But he has also unusual power of hearing: this is because he loved, in some former birth, to listen to the preaching of the Law.'[1] For there is not a balance struck, as might be supposed, between the total good and evil of a man's life or lives; every individual act works out its own reward or punishment independently in its own good time. 'A good man who has once uttered a slander may spend a hundred thousand years as a god in consequence of his goodness, and when the power of his good actions is exhausted, may be born as a dumb man on account of his transgression; and a robber who has once done an act of mercy, may come to life in a king's body as the result of his virtue, and then suffer torments for ages in hell . . . or be reborn many times as a slave or an outcast, in consequence of his evil life.'[2] 'When good King Bunsari's feet were burned and rubbed with salt by command of his cruel son, that he might not walk, why was the torture inflicted on a man so holy? Because in a previous birth he had walked near a dagoba with his slippers on, and had trodden on a priest's carpet without washing his feet.'[3]

But although so much ingenuity is expended on making the punishment fit the crime, the principles on which the apportionment is made frequently conflict with one another, and the logic is often quite unconvincing. According to one principle, those guilty of crimes of violence are reborn in savage animals; a vain man might be reborn a peacock, and what we sometimes call hoggishness might be punished by rebirth in the body of a hog. But to be a hog is no punishment or degradation *to a hog*, nor is it any blame; it is simply nature. And similarly in the other cases.

[1] Mrs. Rhys Davids, *Buddhism*, p. 100.
[2] Rhys Davids, *Hibbert Lectures*, pp. 84-5.
[3] Quoted by Tylor, *op. cit.*, ii. 10-11.

Hence, unless we suppose a soul with human memories encased in the carcase of the hog, and forced to co-operate in the routine of its swinish existence,[1] the penal purpose of the incarnation entirely fails. But the theory does not claim any such memories of previous lives; their absence in our own case makes the claim too difficult to substantiate. This consideration seems fatal, therefore, to the whole idea of punishment by degradation to lower forms of animal life.

Apart from such criticism in detail, it will hardly be claimed that the theory is experimentally verifiable. But certainly with such a belief no one could inveigh, like Huxley, against the 'fathomless injustice of the nature of things'. The Book of Job, it has been said, could never have been written on Indian soil; for moral retribution, functioning as a natural law and calling for no divine intervention to enforce it, is treated there as the inner heart of the world-process. Karma is, in fact, the Indian answer to all such perplexities as to the apparent disregard of moral considerations in the distribution of happiness and misery in the present life. It is undoubtedly, in its general outline, a striking conception; and its impressiveness is vouched for by the hold it has maintained for more than two thousand years over so many millions of the human race. Its main appeal is to what Professor Rhys Davids calls 'the overpowering sense of the necessity of justice'.[2]

But we may ask whether, on a nearer scrutiny, the satisfaction which it yields to that sense is not more imaginary than real. If punishment is to be justified in a juridical sense, the punishment must be borne by the individual who did the wrong; only if he can consciously connect

[1] Like the followers of Odysseus transformed by the magic arts of Circe: 'they had the head and voice, the bristles and the shape of swine, but their mind abode even as beforetime' (*Od.* x. 239–40).

[2] *Hibbert Lectures*, p. 94.

the punishment with the crime, can the suffering have its remedial and purifying effect. Now, as we have seen, great stress is laid, in statements of the doctrine, on the sameness of the individual who reaps with him who sowed. That is, in fact, the essence of the theory and gives it its appeal. But, apart from memory, the successive lives, A, B, C, etc., in which Karma works itself out, are connected only by the figment of a soul-substance, *x*, underlying the series. The existence of such a soul-substance we saw to be unmeaning. But even if we assumed its existence, the individuals A, B, C are, in the absence of memory, juridically separate persons, and the satisfaction gained by punishing B for the faults of A is an illusion of the imagination; any other whipping-boy would do as well. The illusion is still more patent in the Buddhistic version of the theory, for there we are not even asked to believe in the identity of the successive individuals. Buddha discarded altogether the notion of a substantial soul. But, somewhat inconsistently it would almost seem, he retained the doctrine of Karma; and it has remained as central in the religion he founded as it is in Brahmanism. According to his teaching, nothing survives the death of the individual except his Karma, that is to say, the results, good or bad, of his actions—the sum of merit or demerit which he has amassed; and this concentrates itself in the production of 'a new sentient being' whose nature and destiny it determines.[1] The theory, says Prof. Rhys Davids, rests on the one hand on the necessity of justice, on the other on the law of causality; but the Buddhists 'have failed to see that the very key-stone itself, the link between one life and another, is a mere word—this wonderful hypothesis, the individualized and individualizing force of Karma'.[2]

So far as he thinks clearly and in accordance with the

[1] Mrs. Rhys Davids, *Buddhism*, pp. 103–4. [2] *Hibbert Lectures*, pp. 105–6.

doctrines of his faith, the Buddhist thus acknowledges that the so-called reincarnate self is really a new being. The purely imaginary nature of the connexion between the successive lives comes out no less clearly in Mrs. Rhys Davids's sympathetic presentation of the doctrine. The pious Buddhist believes, she says,[1] 'that because of what he is now doing, some one, now in process of mental creation by him, and to all intents and purposes his future self, will one day taste less or more of life's trials'; his present acts are making 'a happy or a miserable successor', although he has no 'definite belief as to how or in what realm of the universe he will arise as that successor to his present self'. Apart from the imaginative concentration upon a single individual, how does this differ, it may be asked, from the Positivist attitude hymned by George Eliot in 'The Choir Invisible', or from the aspiration of any good parent and citizen that his children may have a better chance than he had, not only, or mainly, in worldly things, but also in the things of the mind and the spirit, and his determination that the world, or that part of it for which he is responsible, shall be on the whole a better place for his having lived in it? And, to return to our series of successive lives, if B accepts his chastisement in a religiously submissive spirit as due to the misdeeds of a hypothetical A, of whom and of whose doings he has no knowledge, does his attitude greatly differ from that of the Christian who accepts affliction in the same spirit, from a profound sense of his own shortcomings and those of his race?

I would go farther and venture to challenge the whole conception of moral forces as working along uncommunicating lines in this fashion, each hypothetical series of lives being as it were self-contained, inheriting only its own deeds and expiating only its own sins. This seems to me a defect at once in religious feeling and in speculative imagination. For

[1] *Op. cit.*, p. 148.

we are all members of one body; and although vicarious suffering, in a judicial or legal sense, is nothing less than immoral, the redemptive suffering of the best is the deepest truth of religious experience. So the Apostle does not think of his sufferings for the brethren's sake as an injustice to himself to be hereafter made good: he rejoices in them as 'filling up' 'that which is behind of the afflictions of Christ... for his body's sake, which is the church'.[1] The defectiveness of the conception of Karma is borne out, one might argue, by what the adherents of the doctrine tell us of its working. There is, so far as we can gather from their accounts, nothing redemptive in its operation. The whole emphasis is laid on retribution, and the process becomes an endless one, leading to no goal of ultimate release or consummation. The theory is, says Deussen,[2] 'that life, in quality as well as in quantity, is the accurately meted and altogether fitting expiation of the deeds of a previous existence. But the life in which the expiation takes place necessarily involves further actions, and these afford fresh opportunities for errors, unwitting offences, and sins: and such deeds must be expiated anew in a subsequent existence, so that the clockwork of requital, in running down, always winds itself up again, and so in perpetuity.' Accumulation of merit may help to ease a future life, but can never suffice to effect a release from the weary wheel of endless becoming. Even the great conflagration in which Indian philosophy believes that the present universe will be consumed has no power over the accumulated Karma waiting to produce its effects. A new world-age will follow, not, however, with a clean balance-sheet to start with; for the operation of Karma will proceed in the new age just from the point where it was suspended at the close of the former aeon.

[1] Colossians i. 24.

[2] *System des Vedanta*, pp. 381–2 (quoted by Professor Hogg).

Release, the fixed desire of all Indian thought, can only be achieved by the knowledge or illumination which comes suddenly, and as it were by the grace of God—the vision of the oneness of the self with Brahma which comes to the few, and which, though it cannot arrest their present existence (because that is conditioned by the deeds of a previous life), ensures that, at its close, those who have attained such knowledge escape from phenomenal existence and are made one with Brahma. It is significant, I think, of the failure of Karma to plumb the depths of religious experience that deliverance comes thus from another quarter. Deussen and others have not failed to remark the parallel between the Christian doctrine of salvation by faith and the Vedantic doctrine of redemption by knowledge. Emancipation from the finite, a hopeless quest along the path of works, comes in a moment from the sense of unity with the divine, gained in a supreme experience. The same thing is true of Buddhism. Karma simply perpetuates the curse of existence. Deliverance can come only through such enlightenment as came to the Buddha himself under the Bo tree on the day when he made the 'great renunciation'.

The main appeal of Karma to the modern mind is its insistence on the fact that cause and effect are as inseparably linked in the moral sphere as science assumes them to be in the physical. Every action has its intrinsic consequences for good or for evil; the good effects of a good action and the bad effects of a bad action are not attached to them by any external divine sanction, but follow from the nature of the acts themselves. The sequence is, in short, a natural law, whose operation cannot be evaded. The suggested affinity with scientific law, as opposed to arbitrary enactment, is constantly referred to in sympathetic expositions of the doctrine by European writers. And it is true that the doctrine had its origin in the desire for a rationalistic and purely ethical explanation of the facts of life, in opposition to the complicated mass of superstitious beliefs in the efficacy of sacrifices, penances, ascetic practices, and ritual purifications to turn aside the effects of actions. Buddhism, in particular, employs the doctrine as an emphatic protest against the whole apparatus of priestcraft. Actions have their intrinsic nature and their inevitable consequences; and these cannot be bought off by vain oblations and gifts, by washing in the Ganges, or even by repentance, however sincere. All this, it need hardly be said, is both true and valuable. But if we analyse the real facts of moral causation, we shall not easily extract from them the law that 'everywhere and always the righteous act brings to the doer happiness, the wicked act unhappiness'[1]—in the sense at least in which the Karma system understands these terms. The inevitable consequences of an evil action, or of a course of evil persisted in, is that progressive deterioration of the soul of which Plato speaks in the famous passage of the *Theaetetus* already quoted in an earlier lecture.[2] But such degeneracy, if it be not connected with physical excesses, does not necessarily bring 'unhappiness', in the usual sense of the word, to the doer, though it may cause untold suffering in others. The nature, as it becomes more ingrainedly selfish, becomes more and more insensible to disturbing qualms of conscience or pangs of remorse. Moral causation in any deeper sense—in any verifiable sense—is surely this propagation of goodness by goodness or of evil by evil, primarily in the agent himself, and through him in others. 'He that soweth to the flesh shall of the flesh reap corruption; but he that soweth to the spirit shall of the spirit reap life everlasting.' Payment is in kind. That is 'the principle of the spiritual harvest'.[3]

[1] Mrs. Rhys Davids, *op. cit.*, p. 126. [2] p. 54 *supra*.
[3] Cf. Frederick Robertson's sermon 'The Spiritual Harvest'.

Karma, however, interprets happiness or unhappiness quite frankly in the sense of material well-being and physical suffering. A good deed, according to the doctrine, not only tends to make the agent, and those he is brought into contact with, morally better—not only tends also in most cases to promote the happiness of others—it brings inevitably to the doer, as his recompense, a proportionate amount of agreeable living in some future earthly existence or in some heavenly paradise. An evil action not only inflicts suffering upon others and moral deterioration on the agent, but carries with it, for the latter, penal sufferings in the future exactly commensurate to the offence. This linkage of cause and effect is notoriously not verifiable in the present life; just on that account, indeed, in the name of absolute justice, Karma postulates an infinite succession of lives in which the equation may be established. It cannot, therefore, be regarded as an induction from observed facts and, in that sense, a law scientifically established. The relation between an action and such reward or punishment is neither a seen necessity of reason nor a uniformly observed connexion in nature. Although no divine law-giver is invoked as the author of the arrangement, the alleged consequences are quite as much external sanctions of the acts, as they are, for example, in the Kantian adjustment of happiness to virtue. 'The distribution of happiness in exact proportion to morality constitutes', said Kant, 'the *summum bonum* of a possible world.' Karma is just Kant's third Postulate of the practical reason, put forward as a religious theory of the actual world. The scientific analogy pressed by the advocates of Karma is therefore illusory. The belief rests entirely on the religious or ethical postulate of absolute justice. Retribution is, according to Karma, the essential business of the world; the cosmic process continues to exist for no other purpose than to keep the balance true; and, as the balance is continually being disturbed, the process is interminable.

Retribution is extended in the theory so as to cover rewards as well as punishments; but the ordinary associations of the word are with punishment, and punishment was no doubt the primary, as it tends to continue the most vital, idea in all such theories. Justice itself, for primitive thought—and for a great deal of thought that is not primitive—is mainly concerned with punishment. The idea of justice arises in primitive communities as a legalized revenge, in which the community steps in to supersede private blood-feuds, by sanctioning definite reparation for definite offences, which are henceforth regarded as offences against the community or the community's god. 'To me belongeth vengeance and recompense', we read in the Mosaic law. In view of the stress laid upon the exact proportion of the punishment and the crime, Karma may be said to found its moral universe upon this primitive *lex talionis*. A man's lot is meted out to him according to the measure with which he has meted to others in a former life. The brutish man and the oppressor is born as a slave or low-placed animal, and will suffer all the wrongs and indignities which he himself previously inflicted upon others.[1] The doctrine seems open, therefore, to all the criticism to which the vindictive theory of punishment has been subjected in modern times, and to which in most quarters it has succumbed. It is now generally recognized, in law and in education, that punishment is not an end in itself. The idea of punishment for the sake of punishment is as barren as the idea

[1] Plato, it may be noted, gives precisely the same account of the teaching of 'those learned in the mysteries'. 'They say that the crime will be punished in the world below, and also that when the perpetrators return to this world *they will suffer what they did by a compensation of nature*, and [murderers] will end their lives in like manner by the hand of another' (*Laws*, 870).

of specific reward for each virtuous act is unworthy; and to conceive this wonderful universe as primarily a place for the doling out of punishment is to degrade it to the level of a glorified police-court. 'Master, who did sin, this man, or his parents, that he was born blind?' It is not fanciful, I think, to detect almost a gesture of impatience in the way both suggestions are brushed aside, and with them the unfounded and all-too-mechanical view of the Divine working in which they had their rise.

Yet the system of Karma and reincarnation has still a certain fascination for contemporary thinkers as an explanation of what is sometimes called the moral indifference of nature. Thus Mr. Edmond Holmes, in his sincere and attractive autobiographical volume, called *The Quest of an Ideal*,[1] says, 'With the doctrine of reincarnation, the doctrine of Karma came into my life and found a ready welcome in my heart. The conception of an all-controlling law of natural retribution which links together the successive earth-lives of each individual soul, both satisfied my sense of justice and threw light on the problem of seemingly unmerited suffering—unmerited or only partly merited—the problem which has appealed so strongly to the master-singers of the world, the makers of tragedy.' But is his diagnosis of the problem and the solution really correct? 'The inspired poet', he proceeds, 'finds that success (or what passes as such)—that happiness (or what passes as such)—is no fit subject for artistic treatment; that suffering alone can inspire him, and that the suffering must be in large measure unmerited, if the story of it is to rise to the level of genuine poetry. And yet, strange as it may seem, when he sings of failure, he does not move us to despair. We feel, when the failure has been consummated, that the darkness is akin to that which precedes the dawn;

[1] p. 98.

we feel that a mysterious error has been atoned for: that mighty forces, whose false starts and arrested movements count for more than our most splendid successes, are free to resume their advance. So, too, when the poet makes his hero suffer far in excess of his deserts, our sense of justice is in no wise outraged. On the contrary, we feel that the suffering has a meaning and a scope which make our mundane notions of justice wholly inapplicable to it; we feel that it is balanced somewhere and somehow by some high demand, some deep necessity, some far-reaching result.' 'The doctrine of Karma', he concludes, 'explains and justifies this feeling.' To me it seems, on the contrary, that in these illuminative sentences on tragedy and the nature of the tragic emotion Mr. Holmes has left Karma far behind him, or has transformed it into something larger and truer than its actual self; for is not Karma precisely the apotheosis of 'our mundane notions of justice', eliminating the very idea of tragedy, and with it much of the dignity and greatness of the world?[1]

A still more signal instance may be quoted of the confusion of thought which sometimes leads a man to welcome the idea of Karma because he mistakes it for its very opposite. Perhaps the longest book ever written on Immortality is Alger's *History of the Doctrine of a Future Life.* In his final review of the subject, written five years later than the main body of the work, the author shows a certain disposition to favour the theory of reincarnation, and this is the astound-

[1] Cf. A. C. Bradley, *Shakespearean Tragedy*, pp. 32-3: 'The ideas of justice and desert are, it seems to me, in *all* cases untrue to our imaginative experience.... This is a point of view which emerges only where, in reading a play, we slip, by our own fault or the dramatist's, from the tragic position, or when, in thinking about the play afterwards, we fall back on our everyday legal and moral notions. But tragedy does not belong, any more than religion belongs, to the sphere of these notions: neither does the imaginative attitude in presence of it.' Cf. also the analysis of tragic emotion on pp. 324-5.

ing reason he gives: 'Then every suffering we endure *for faults not our own, the consequence of the deeds of others,* assumes a holy light and a sublime dignity, associating us with that great sacrifice of atoning pain, whereof the crucified Christ is not the exclusive instance, but the representative head.' The italics are mine, for surely the law of Karma is more correctly stated by another European adherent of a different mental type, to whom it appeals, in her own words, as 'the only perfect justice'. 'In it we see that each soul suffers precisely according to its sins; *no one suffers for the sins of another.* When men are born to suffering, it is because in past lives they have deserved it.'[1] Yet so little are people aware of what it really is in their beliefs that touches their imagination and yields them religious sustenance, that the significance of Karma for Eastern thought may lie, after all, not in the idea of the identity of the empirical individual and the abstract justice which pursues him through successive lives, but in the individual's feeling of his oneness with the generations of the past whom he has neither seen nor known. Certainly it appears, from the instances I have quoted and from many others, that for its modern European votaries it is not the mechanical idea of an identical soul-substance passing from body to body, but the mystical idea of suffering with and for others, that forms the real attraction of the doctrine. And perhaps that may be the true explanation of its long ascendancy in the East as well.

Quite apart from the doctrine of Karma, it is sometimes maintained that the future immortality of the soul implies its pre-existence, and that it is illogical to believe in the one unless we accept the other also. Such a conclusion apparently depends on the assumption that whatever has

[1] Quoted by Miss Dougall in her essay on 'Reincarnation, Karma and Theosophy' in the volume, *Immortality*, edited by Canon Streeter.

a beginning will also have an end. If so, only that can be expected to persist unendingly which is literally and inherently self-subsistent. This is the position taken up by Dr. McTaggart, one of the comparatively few philosophers who put the doctrine of immortality in the forefront of their system. He believes, he tells us, 'that any evidence which will prove immortality will also prove pre-existence'.[1] This somewhat surprising statement becomes intelligible when we find him dismissing the usual ethical arguments as inconclusive and taking his stand on 'the purely metaphysical arguments' as alone capable of yielding *a priori* certainty. For the sole argument on which he founds is that 'the self is a substance existing in its own right'; and, according to his developed theory, the universe consists, in the last analysis, of a society of such eternally self-subsistent selves. If we define all selves as substances in this sense, it follows at once that they have neither beginning of days nor end of life. We are bound to conclude, as Dr. McTaggart says, that 'each of us exists through all time—past and future'.[2] And inasmuch as in the present life we have no memory of any previous existence, we must assume a 'plurality of lives', cut off from one another by successive deaths and rebirths.

Dr. McTaggart's metaphysical argument seems, as I have said, to rest entirely on his definition of the self; and the definition, I am bound to say, seems to me no better than a dogma. We saw reason, in the preceding lecture, to regard the self as characterized by a unity and coherence greater than, and different in kind from, that exhibited by any material thing. As self-conscious, it seemed to round itself to a separate whole in a sense in which that could not be asserted of any other form of being known to us. If, then, we were inclined to use what Dr. McTaggart admits

[1] *Some Dogmas of Religion*, p. 113.
[2] *Ibid.*, p. 115.

to be the 'unfashionable' term, substance, we might say that the self or soul was eminently entitled to that designation. But if we did so use the term, we should mean thereby to describe the observed mode of behaviour of the self, not to lay down *a priori* the necessary conditions of its being and duration. We know that it possesses a certain kind and degree of unity and coherence within certain limits of time open to our observation. But the unity and coherence appear to be a gradual growth within our experience; and, even when attained in the fullest measure, they furnish us with no abstract guarantee that the systematic whole thus constituted will continue to hold together and maintain itself for ever. But Dr. McTaggart's use of the term substance (though he tries to safeguard himself) inevitably carries us back to the discredited soul-substance which we have so fully criticized. The substance in which, he says, the personal identity lies,[1] serves only as an unknown metaphysical substrate which is supposed to link the separate life-histories together. The continuity of the successive lives is never realized in consciousness, owing to the absence of memory; but Dr. McTaggart supposes this substrate to form, as it were, the vehicle by which mental and moral qualities acquired by an individual in the course of a single life may be transmitted to the next incarnation, to be his working capital and the starting-point, possibly, of further advance. Now it is, of course, beyond question that countless items of our experience lapse, within the present life, from conscious memory, and survive only as aptitudes, dispositions, and tendencies. Our personality is not exhausted, therefore, by the individual experiences we can consciously recall. But although much may persist in this subconscious fashion, some continuity of conscious memory is undoubtedly involved in

[1] 'In the identity of the substance lies, it seems to me, the personal identity' (*Studies in Hegelian Cosmology*, p. 37).

the ordinary notion of personality; and therefore it is paradoxical, and to the ordinary mind misleading, when Dr. McTaggart asserts that 'in spite of the loss of memory it is the same person who lives in the successive lives'. The identity does not exist for any one of the successive incarnations. Each self is the realized unity of a single life, and it is unmeaning, therefore, to speak of two such self-contained lives as the experiences of the same person or self.

Sometimes an acknowledgement of the ambiguity creeps into Dr. McTaggart's phraseology, just as we found it doing in the case of the Buddhists; as, for example, when he asks whether a man, on being assured that he would presently lose all memory of his past, would consider that to be annihilation, and 'take no more interest in *the person of a similar character* who would occupy his old body than he would in a stranger'. If I were to reply to this question, I could only point out that, in any case, the interest thus projected into the future must be the sentimental curiosity of an imaginary onlooker. But the question recalls (and was perhaps suggested by) the similar interrogation with which Leibniz clinches his criticism of the Cartesian immortality of substance: 'Granting that the soul is a substance and that no substance perishes, the soul then will not be lost, as, indeed, nothing is lost in nature. . . . But this immortality without recollection is ethically quite useless. . . . What good, sir, would it do you to become King of China, on condition that you forget what you have been? Would it not be the same as if God, at the moment he destroyed you, were to create a king in China?'[1] As regards the point in dispute, I am content to let the earlier question answer the later. Only an illusion of the imagination permits us to speak of immortality where there is no memory to maintain the identity of what Mr. Bradley

[1] Leibniz, *Philosophische Schriften* (Gerhardt), iv. 300.

terms 'the felt self',[1] or allows us to offer in exchange for such personal immortality a succession of what Dr. McTaggart himself calls 'separate lives'.

Nevertheless, the idea of these successive lives is evidently to Dr. McTaggart a source of elevated and consoling thoughts, for it moves him from time to time to a passage of mystical beauty. Take the following, which exemplifies his feeling, and also, I must contend, the persistent illusion on which the emotion rests: 'Death is not a haven of rest. It is a starting-point for fresh labours. But if the trials are great, so is the recompense. We miss much here by our own folly, much by unfavourable circumstances. Above all, we miss much because so many good things are incompatible. We cannot spend our youth both in the study and in the saddle. We cannot gain the benefit both of unbroken health and of bodily weakness, both of riches and of poverty, both of comradeship and of isolation, both of defiance and of obedience. We cannot learn the lessons alike of Galahad and of Tristram and of Caradoc. And yet they are all so good to learn. Would it not be worth much to be able to hope that what we missed in one life might come to us in another? And would it not be worth much to be able to hope that we might have a chance to succeed hereafter in the tasks which we failed in here? . . . Though the way is long, and perhaps endless, it can be no more wearisome than a single life. For with death we leave behind us memory, and old age, and fatigue. And surely death acquires a new and deeper significance when we regard it no longer as a single and unexplained break in an unending life, but as part of the continually recurring rhythm of progress—as inevitable, as natural, and as benevolent as sleep. We have only left youth behind us,

[1] Cf. *Essays on Truth and Reality*, p. 453 *et seq.*

as at noon we have left the sunrise. They will both come back, and they do not grow old.'[1]

Every reader will feel the sustained beauty of the words; the illusion lies in the recurrent 'we' and 'us'. Otherwise the idea of supplementing and enlarging our limited earthly experience is a natural and attractive one. But it is a prospect equally open to the ordinary believer in personal immortality; and in his case the enrichment of the personality would be real, whereas on Dr. McTaggart's theory, the varied experiences remain distributed among a number of different individuals. Galahad knows nothing of Tristram, nor Tristram of Galahad, nor either of them anything of Caradoc, nor Caradoc of either. So, again, it is good to rejoice that 'the sunrise with its glories old' will gladden young eyes and hearts ages after our own eyes have closed in death, but it is an illusion to think that it is we who shall look through their eyes or feel the beat of their hearts.

Before we leave the theory of reincarnation it may not be amiss to add a few words in criticism of the curious underlying assumption of a determinate number of souls. 'The souls that exist', says Plato, 'must be always the same. They cannot become fewer, nor yet can they become more numerous.'[2] In the *Timaeus* he says their number is equal to the number of the stars,[3] and the statement is not to be taken as a metaphorical expression for the infinite or innumerable. Plutarch, in one of his Symposiacs, debated the question whether the total number of the stars is more probably odd or even. For Dr. McTaggart also the selves are 'fundamental differentiations' of the Absolute, determinate in nature and in number. 'It is the nature of the Absolute to be manifested in precisely those differentiations in which it is

[1] *Some Dogmas of Religion*, pp. 138–9.
[2] *Republic*, 611.
[3] *Timaeus*, 41.

manifested.'[1] Mr. Bradley, from his own point of view, takes up a similar position. 'There is one sense', he says, 'in which the immortality of souls seems impossible. We must remember that the universe is incapable of increase. And to suppose a constant supply of new souls, none of which ever perished, would clearly land us in the end in an insoluble difficulty.'[2]

But why this penurious economy in souls or substances? Is it not because our conception of substance is drawn originally from the physical world and refuses to let us escape from the associations of the unchanging atom? Modern physics has transformed the atom out of knowledge, but the laws of the conservation of matter and the conservation of energy still express the same presupposition. The physicist operates within a closed system, and his equations represent transformations within that system—transformations of that which remains quantitatively identical with itself. It seems to me that it is from physics we derive the notion of reality as a fixed quantum, which can neither be increased nor diminished; and, applying this to the spiritual life, we arrive at the idea of a fixed number of souls undergoing perpetual transmigrations. But, once more, the science of life offers itself as a truer guide to the nature of the spiritual facts. For in contrast to the cycles of physical change, returning upon themselves, life exhibits the world to us as a process of what may not unjustly be called *creative* evolution —a striving after the better, which achieves the production of what is really new. Biology too, as we saw, introduces us for the first time to the real individual. It is contrary to the whole suggestion of the biological facts to suppose a definite number of souls, whether self-existent or (as in some theories) originally created by God *en gros*. Surely, if we profess a rational Theism, we shall think of the

[1] *Hegelian Cosmology*, p. 31. Cf. p. 9: 'The whole meaning and significance of the unity lies in its being differentiated into that particular plurality.'

[2] *Appearance and Reality*, p. 502.

whole evolutionary process as a continuous creation by natural means; and on such a view everything should lead us to accept the *prima facie* suggestion of the facts—that each human birth is a fresh creation, the advent of what, when the shaping forces of the years have done their work, will be a conscious personality, in the strictest sense unique. Reincarnation, it has been said by a woman critic, 'makes childhood, which appears so beautiful and so holy as the beginning of a virgin soul, a gigantic lie. It is hard to conceive how any mother can look into the dawning intelligence of her child's eyes, and be satisfied to believe that in innumerable past lives that same soul has gone through experience savage and civilized, has probably been in turn harlot or rake, victim or tyrant, wife or warrior, layman or priest, and perhaps all these a hundred times.'[1]

And again, if we free our minds from physical analogies, the fact that the spiritual unity of the self is essentially a new creation constitutes in itself no reason why, after a certain term, it should necessarily cease to exist; for it is not as if it were a compound of pre-existing elements into which it must be again resolved. Equally, of course, the mere fact of its emergence constitutes no guarantee of an endless destiny. That may be an issue placed in its own hands. But unless we are possessed by Abraham Tucker's quaint idea that 'the number of souls daily pouring in from hence upon the next world would seem to require a proportionable drain from it somewhere or other, for else the country might be overstocked',[2] we need not be driven to the theory of reincarnation to obviate this lamentable result. Such Malthusian anxieties about the over-population of the spiritual world appear at once ludicrous and presumptuous in beings like ourselves.

[1] Miss Dougall, in the essay already quoted, *Immortality*, p. 301.
[2] *Light of Nature Pursued*, vol. iii, p. 361.

LECTURE VII

ETERNAL LIFE

In the theory of Karma, reincarnation is not put forward as the goal of desire. So much at least will be evident from the discussion in the preceding lecture. Christian writers are accustomed to speak of 'the hope of immortality', and theologians frequently use the phrase 'a blessed immortality'; but, for the millions who really believe in it, reincarnation is not a 'hope', it is rather, one might say, a 'doom' to which they must submit. It is explicitly part of the wheel of becoming; and the endlessness of the process, instead of being an attraction ('On and always on', as Tennyson says), operates on the imagination like a nightmare. The sustaining hope is that, after the lapse of ages, release from the wheel may be attained, that is to say, the cessation of finite or separate being, either by absorption into Brahma or, as it would seem in Buddhism, by actual extinction. It is obvious, therefore, that if we mean by immortality simply an endless continuance of our individual existence, opinions may differ as to the desirability of such a gift or endowment.

Twenty years ago the American Branch of the Society for Psychical Research issued a *questionnaire* on 'Human Sentiment with regard to a Future Life', and the first two questions were:

(1) Would you prefer to live after death or not?

(2) If you would prefer to live after death, do you desire a future life whatever the conditions might be, or, if that is not so, what would have to be its character to make the prospect seem tolerable?

The replies received were not very instructive and

perhaps not sufficiently representative,[1] but Plutarch has left us his answers to the precise terms of these two questions, and he professes to speak for the vast majority of mankind. 'The hope of eternity and the yearning for life', he writes, 'is the oldest, as it is the greatest, of human desires.' 'I might almost say that all men and women would readily submit themselves to the teeth of Cerberus, and to the punishment of carrying water in a sieve, if only they might remain in existence and escape the doom of annihilation.'[2] Milton has put the same sentiment in the mouth of one of the rebel angels contemplating the alternative of annihilation in an access of the divine wrath.[3] But the nearest modern parallel to Plutarch's passage is perhaps to be found in Heine's lines shortly before his death; and the force of the feeling they represent will be best realized if we remember that they were written from the 'mattress-grave' in Paris, where he had lingered for so many years:

> O Gott, wie hässlich bitter ist das Sterben!
> O Gott, wie süss und traulich lässt sich's leben
> In diesem traulich süssen Erdennest!

The words recall Claudio's passionate recoil from the thought of impending death in *Measure for Measure*:

> This sensible warm motion to become
> A kneaded clod.

But Claudio's ignoble dread, like Hamlet's hesitation, is due not to the idea of extinction, but to 'what we fear of death', 'what dreams may come'.

> The weariest and most loathèd worldly life
> That age, ache, penury, and imprisonment
> Can lay on nature, is a paradise
> To what we fear of death.

[1] That is, on the whole, Dr. Schiller's opinion of the statistical results which he published in the *Proceedings of the Society for Psychical Research*, vol. xviii (1903).

[2] *Non posse suaviter vivi secundum Epicurum*, 1104.

[3] *Paradise Lost*, ii. 146–51.

Heine was not troubled by such fears: it was just th blankness of death that wrung the words from him. 'Hov our soul struggles against the thought of the cessation o our personality, of eternal annihilation! The *horror vacu* which we ascribe to nature is really inborn in the huma heart.' So he had written some years earlier in the wel known postscript to his *Romanzero*. Yet the attitud which these two writers so vehemently express is certainl not universal. We have just seen how widely divergen is the voice of Eastern philosophy and Eastern religion As it has been neatly put, the width of the divergenc between East and West may be estimated from the fac that 'the destiny which in one hemisphere has been pro pounded as the final reward of virtue is regarded in th other as the extreme penalty of obstinate wickedness'. Where the theory of annihilation has found favour i Christian circles, its acceptance has usually been due t a recoil from the thought of the eternal duration of futur punishment. But the profound weariness and sense o oppression, which the thought of the endlessness of futur existence is capable of engendering, is not confined to th East. In the West, too, it is found prompting the hope—

> That even the weariest river
> Winds somewhere safe to sea.[2]

Eternal rest is the deepest longing of many an over-drive body and tortured soul.

> Sleep after toil, port after stormy seas,
> Ease after war, death after life, does greatly please.

Buddha avowedly links his doctrine to the though of the suffering or sorrow which accompanies all finit existence, and Brahmanism emphasizes the emptiness the illusory character of the finite. But it is not merel

[1] Article on 'Annihilation' by Rev. G. C. Joyce in Hastings's *Encyclo paedia of Religion and Ethics*.

[2] Swinburne, 'Garden of Proserpine'.

[3] *Faerie Queen*, Bk. I. ix. 40.

he pessimism of Eastern thought that underlies its view
ere. Perhaps we should not be wrong in saying that
he East is naturally more speculative than the West,
nd therefore thinks out and realizes more fully the
mplications of a metaphysical idea like that of endlessness. The Western temperament, with its active bias,
s content for the most part to take the doctrine of im-
nortality pragmatically, as equivalent to the belief that
leath does not end all, without developing its further
consequences. Only, perhaps, in connexion with the doc-
rine of eternal punishment has there been any vivid
attempt to realize and to apply these consequences. The
unendingness of the penal fire was a theme on which
preachers loved to dilate as embodying a horror greater
even than the cruelty of the tortures depicted.

Questi non hanno speranza di morte

is one of Dante's most terrible lines. Yet it does not require the experience of the damned to produce this sense of intolerableness. It is sufficient to concentrate our thoughts, or we might better say our imagination, on mere endlessness or pure succession. A personal immortality, so conceived, instead of being felt as a state of blessedness, oppresses us like a burden too heavy to be borne. 'Is it *never* to end?' [I quote one homely utterance.] 'The thought appals. I, little I, to live a million years—and another million—and another! My tiny light to burn for ever.'[1] We did not require, in short, to wait for Hegel to tell us that the endless progress in time or in space is the false infinite. The feeling is instinctive. It is the aimlessness of the process which afflicts the mind; for it is a progress which leads nowhere, which has no goal, seeing that, after ages of forward movement, you are precisely as distant from the imagined end as when you started.

[1] Quoted by Dr. S. H. Mellone, *The Immortal Hope*, p. 6.

But this impression is produced, it will be said, only be cause we allow ourselves to be gorgonized by the idea o empty time and the endless succession of its moments, apart from the experiences which fill them. As each moment of time, looked at thus abstractly, is exactly like every other, progress inevitably appears as a change which is nc change. But if we think of the content of our experiences it is argued, the afflicting illusion will disappear. In thinking of an immortal life we may, and ought to, think of it, not as the simple continuance of a being in existence at the same level of all his powers and attainments, but as a progress or advance in a real sense, a continuous growth towards the stature of a perfect humanity. The idea of growth, it is urged, liberates us from the oppressiveness of an unchanging identity. With ever new insights opened to us, and ever new conquests achieved, there can be no question of existence palling upon the taste. In the nature of things, the process can have no end; but, absorbed in each stage as it opens before us, we need not be distracted by the empty thought of the series of future stages still to be traversed. The future, in such a case, would not break upon us until it was present. It is clear, I think, that we are here on the road to a more satisfactory theory, but the improvement lies rather in the stress laid on the quality of the experiences than on the idea of growth as such. Kant's argument for the immortality of the soul based on the conception of the moral life as an infinite process of approximation to perfect virtue, might, I suppose, be taken as a typical application, from the ethical side, of the idea of growth. But such a process is still perilously like the *progressus in indefinitum*; it has, indeed, often been attacked on that ground. The infinite distance of the goal—nay, its explicit unreachableness—is the thought which inspires the argument; and hence the spectre of the future is inevitably conjured up with all the tension of the time-process. Unless we can rise to some experience satisfying in itself, we are not likely to reach a tenable theory of immortality. And, if we are to realize such an experience, we must pass beyond morality to religion, in which the life of finite struggle and endeavour is somehow transcended—where we escape, therefore, from the implications of the time-process, of which the moral life, in the strict sense of the word, is the typical expression.

Accordingly we find both theologians and philosophers insisting on the idea of an 'eternal life', not as something in the future, a continuance of existence after our earthly life is ended, but as an experience, a state of being, to be enjoyed here and now. So, for example, in Schleiermacher's famous declaration: 'The goal and the character of the religious life is not the immortality desired and believed in by many. . . . It is not the immortality that is outside of time, behind it or rather after it, and which still is in time. It is the immortality which we can have now in this temporal life. In the midst of finitude to be one with the Infinite, and in every moment to be eternal, that is the immortality of religion.'[1] The idea is very commonly put forward, as it is in this passage of Schleiermacher's, in opposition to banal and selfishly personal conceptions of a future life, which have nothing religious about them; and hence such statements are often interpreted as implying that the enjoyment of the eternal life described is limited to the opportunities afforded by the present life. They are taken as definitely negating the idea of personal immortality in any ordinary sense of the term. This negative attitude is, no doubt, adopted by many: they put forward the possibility of realizing eternal life here and now *in place of* the further life which we ordinarily mean by immortality.

[1] The closing sentences of the second of his *Reden über die Religion.*

Schleiermacher himself, at least during the earlier part of his career, seems to have held such a view. There is recounted in Dr. Martineau's *Study of Religion*[1] the touching story of his ineffectual efforts to console a young widow whose husband, according to Schleiermacher's teaching, had 'melted away into the great All'. But eternity and immortality are by no means necessarily exclusive terms: on the contrary, our experience here and now may carry in it 'the power of an endless life', and be in truth the only earnest or guarantee of such a life.

It is a commonplace of philosophical criticism that the term 'eternal', when strictly and properly used, does not mean endless continuance *in* time, but a quality of experience which transcends time altogether. Thus in Spinoza, where the contrast is specially emphasized, eternity means rational necessity. We know things 'under a certain form of eternity' when we see them not as isolated contingent events, but as necessary parts of a single system, each integral to the whole. It is of the nature of reason (*de natura rationis*) so to regard things, and the perception of this timeless necessity is a very real experience. Mr. Bertrand Russell has told our own generation afresh, in this connexion, that 'mathematics, rightly viewed, possesses not only truth but supreme beauty—a beauty cold and austere like that of sculpture . . . yet sublimely pure, and capable of a stern perfection such as only the greatest art can show. The true spirit of delight, the exaltation, the sense of being more than man, which is the touchstone of the highest excellence, is to be found in mathematics as surely as in poetry.'[2] For Spinoza the necessity of reason is not divorced, as with Mr. Russell, from actual existence. It is Spinoza's vision of the universe as in all its parts a system of divine necessity which creates in him 'the intellectual love of God', that supreme emotion which expels all

[1] ii. 357–60. [2] *Philosophical Essays*, p. 73.

lower or merely selfish desires, because it is itself joy and peace, the perfect satisfaction of the mind (*vera mentis acquiescentia*). 'All our happiness or unhappiness', he tells us, 'depends solely on the quality of the object on which our love is fixed. . . . But love towards an object eternal and infinite feeds the mind with a joy that is pure with no tinge of sadness.'[1] Such is the life of 'thoughts immortal and divine' of which we found Plato and Aristotle also speaking as opening up to the thinker a present immortality.[2] For Spinoza this 'eternal life' is realized in the intellectual vision of truth and harmony; and, as he twice over reminds us in the *Short Treatise*, Truth—the ultimate or all-embracing Truth—is God Himself. This is the 'intuition' (*scientia intuitiva*) in which knowledge culminates.

But Art, or, to put it more widely, the perception of Beauty, also yields us experiences under a similar 'form of eternity'.

> A thing of beauty is a joy for ever:
> Its loveliness increases; it will never
> Pass into nothingness.

Art, it has been said, is the wide world's memory of things. Think only of some of the great stories which have delighted generation after generation, the tale of Troy, the wanderings of Odysseus, the history of Don Quixote. Think of the figures of drama, every turn of whose fate is graven upon our mind and heart, 'forms more real than living man', who trod the boards centuries before our coming, and on whom the curtain will rise as many ages after we have gone. Or take the forms bequeathed to us by the sculptor's art, or some melody of immortal loveliness. Perhaps this sense of bodiless immortality is most vividly realized by the ordinary person

[1] *De Intellectus Emendatione*, sections 9 and 10.

[2] Cf. *supra*, pp. 39–40.

in the case of a musical work, as the sounds fill the air and the instruments give its harmonies and sequences once more a brief existence for the bodily ear.

In Art, as Schopenhauer loved to insist,[1] the objects we contemplate have the eternity and universality of the Platonic Ideas. They are lifted out of the stream of becoming which constitutes individual existence; and in contemplating them we are emancipated from the tyranny of the Will, that is to say, of selfish desire. In aesthetic perception our knowledge is pure and disinterested; our objectivity is complete. 'The subject and the object mutually fill and penetrate each other completely.' Science, based on the principle of causality, is constantly investigating the relations of its object to other things, and is involved, thereby, in an endless quest. 'Art is everywhere at its goal, for it plucks the object of its contemplation out of the world's course, and has it isolated before it. And this particular thing, which in that stream was a small perishing part, becomes to art the representative of the whole, an equivalent of the endless multitude in space and time. The course of time stops; relations vanish for it; only the essential, the Idea, is its object.' Our individuality has fallen from us: 'we are only that *one* eye of the world which looks out from all knowing creatures, but only in man can become perfectly free from the service of the will.' 'Then all at once the peace which we were always seeking, but which fled from us on the former path of the desires, comes to us of its own accord and it is well with us: we keep a Sabbath from the penal slavery of the will; the wheel of Ixion stands still.'[2] Many, accordingly, have celebrated

[1] *The World as Will and Idea*, Bk. III. English translation, vol. i, pp. 219-346.

[2] Schopenhauer speaks mainly of beauty as perceived through the medium of art, but he does not fail to point out that 'a single free glance

Art in this strain, as the only refuge of the spirit from the miseries and weariness of the actual world,

> The weariness, the fever, and the fret,
> Here where men sit and hear each other groan.

To such natures—to Keats, from whom I have quoted, to Goethe and Schiller at certain points in their career—Art thus becomes a religion, or at least is made to do duty for one.[1] Such moments, however, of selfless contemplation and aesthetic enjoyment cannot be more than intermittent, Schopenhauer confesses, and therefore Art cannot achieve that perfect and final deliverance which we seek from the misery of existence. For that we must go, he teaches, to religion, to a religion like Buddhism, which inculcates the resolute extermination of the will to live.

It is in religion, after all, that the term 'eternal life' is most familiar to us. It occurs constantly in the New Testament as the designation of a frame of mind or spiritual attitude which is intended to be realized here and now. The meaning of the phrase in early Christian usage can hardly be fully understood, however, without a glance at the Jewish apocalyptic beliefs, so prominent in men's minds at the time, with which it was at first closely associated, but with which it comes to be in a sense contrasted. We have seen in a previous Lecture how slow was the growth of an effective doctrine of a future life among the Hebrews. When it did arise, it was associated with the national hope of a Messianic kingdom. 'The day of Jahveh', originally conceived simply as a judgement on the enemies of Israel executed by the national god, and the inauguration of a new period of material prosperity under his protection, had been transformed by the prophets into the idea of a day of judgement upon Israel itself for

into nature' may have the same emancipating effect: this is the secret of nature's wonderful restorative and calming power.

[1] Cf. Schiller, *Das Ideal und das Leben*.

the nation's sins; and with the rise of a true monotheism (from the seventh century onwards) this judgement was extended to include all the nations of the earth. The result of the prophesied judgement was to be the establishment of the righteous and penitent remnant of Israel under a prince of the house of David, or a dynasty of such warrior kings and righteous rulers. Other nations—the Gentiles—were either to be destroyed, according to the bitter nationalism of some of the prophets, or, according to the larger-hearted, brought into this divinely established kingdom by conversion. The kingdom was to be set up on this present earth and would last for ever, and the righteous dead of Israel were to be raised from Sheol to participate in its blessedness.[1]

This was the first form of the apocalyptic idea, but in course of time—about the close of the second century B.C.—it came to be realized that the earth (whether as we know it or as transformed into 'a new heaven and a new earth') was unfit to be the scene of such an eternal kingdom: the Kingdom of God could be realized only in a spiritual world to come. The idea of a Messianic reign of the saints upon earth was not abandoned, but it was conceived as temporary in duration (sometimes as lasting a thousand years), and as a prelude to the final judgement which inaugurates the eternal kingdom of God. The important point, however, remains the same, namely, the sharp distinction drawn between 'the present age', in which the powers of wickedness hold sway, and 'the coming age', when the divine kingdom will be realized. The appearance of the Messiah, now

[1] So in Isaiah xxvi. 19, a passage considered by the critics to date from the late Persian period: 'Thy dead shall arise, the inhabitants of the dust shall awake and sing for joy; for a dew of lights is thy dew, and the earth shall produce the shades.' So again, more definitely, in Daniel xii. 2. Formerly it had been believed that the Messianic kingdom would be shared only by the living. Cf. Professor H. R. Mackintosh, *Immortality and the Future*, p. 34. I have adopted Professor Mackintosh's rendering of the passage from Isaiah.

conceived as a supernatural being—'the Son of man' or 'the Son of God'—is the event which is to mark the advent, or at least the near approach, of the new age. Such were the convictions of the religious part of the Jewish nation in the time of Jesus, and this eschatology meets us everywhere in the New Testament. The sense of the imminence of the coming of the Kingdom is universal. 'The Kingdom of Heaven is at hand' was the text of John the Baptist's preaching, and the phrase was appropriated and applied by Jesus in his own way. The first idea which the words roused in the minds of his hearers was the thought of this future dispensation, to be ushered in catastrophically by the appearance of the Messiah on the clouds of heaven to judge the world.[1] Jesus himself appears to have shared the general belief that this event would take place within the life-time of those whom he was addressing: 'There be some standing here which shall not taste of death, till they see the Son of man coming in his Kingdom.'[2] 'This generation shall not pass, till all these things be fulfilled.'[3] When he sent out the Twelve on their preaching mission, he is represented as saying that, before their return, the expected event would have taken place: 'Verily I say unto you, Ye shall not have gone over the cities of Israel, till the Son of man be come.'[4] We need not wonder, therefore, if, in spite of the rest of their Master's teaching about the spiritual nature of the Kingdom, the disciples continued to give his sayings about it this future reference, and had to be rebuked for the thoroughly mundane hopes of reward and distinction which they linked with its establishment.

Yet, from the beginning of his teaching, Jesus made the inheritance of this kingdom dependent on purely spiritual

[1] Or, in the case of those who recognized in Jesus the Messiah or the Christ already come, the *second* coming of the Messiah, in power.

[2] Matt. xvi. 28. [3] Matt. xxiv. 34. [4] Matt. x. 23.

conditions. He taught not simply, like John the Baptist or the prophets before him, that the kingdom of heaven was at hand, but that it was already a present fact—'in their midst' or 'within them'; and, in so doing, he stepped out of the ranks of the Hebrew prophets and came forward as the bearer of a new message from God to man. And the gospel he proclaimed was not a promise of future reward for certain beliefs about himself, but, as every genuinely religious message must be, a gospel of deliverance, a message of present salvation: 'Come unto me, all ye that labour and are heavy laden, and *I will give you rest.* Take my yoke upon you and learn of me; for I am meek and lowly in heart: and *ye shall find rest unto your souls.*'[1] It is an insight which changes the face of the world and 'makes all things new'. Above all it is an insight into what salvation really means. Not a password enabling a man to escape dire penalties in the future or admitting him to great rewards, but a change of the inner man, the adoption of a new attitude towards life and its happenings. The changed attitude is not to be understood as the condition of salvation, in the sense that salvation is something different from the spiritual state and externally added to it. As St. Paul says, 'To be spiritually minded *is* life and peace.'[2] This, then, is the salvation of the soul, the only salvation that matters, as the Platonic Socrates had already so impressively insisted: and when Jesus says 'A man's *life* consisteth not in the abundance of the things which he possesseth',[3] or 'What shall it profit a man if he shall gain the whole world and lose his own *soul*?',[4] the words 'life' and 'soul' are clearly used in the Platonic sense and not in an eschatological reference. Hence we have the antithesis of 'life' and 'death', so recurrent in the New Testament, both terms being used to signify a

[1] Matt. xi. 28–9.
[2] Romans viii. 6.
[3] Luke xii. 15.
[4] Mark viii. 36.

present spiritual state. The message of the Gospel is continually referred to as a message of 'life', and the change it effects is described as a passage from 'death unto life'. The antithesis is equated by St. Paul with his own favourite contrast between the flesh and the spirit. 'To be carnally minded is death; but to be spiritually minded is life and peace.' 'The law of the spirit of life in Christ Jesus hath made me free from the law of sin and death . . . The body is dead because of sin, but the spirit is life because of righteousness.'[1] He also inweaves with his statement that other sense of 'death', contained in the most characteristic teaching of Jesus, that 'whosoever will save his life shall lose it: and whosoever will lose his life for my sake shall find it'.[2] This is, in his own emphatic phrase, the very 'word of the cross',[3] life through death. We must die to self—to selfish desires and egoistic cravings—before we can find our true self in that wider life which is at once the love of the brethren and the love of God.[4] In this sense, St. Paul protests, he dies daily: only by dying with Christ, 'crucifying the flesh with the passions and the lusts thereof',[5] can we share with him the higher life to which he showed the way. As sharing that life, 'walking in Him', 'complete in Him', St. Paul describes believers as already 'risen with Christ'. Thus the death and resurrection of Jesus, which he accepted (we know) as historical facts, and his own resurrection, to which he undoubtedly looked forward as a future event, became for the Apostle, as a religious thinker, a description of the eternal nature of the spiritual life, symbols of an experience daily realized. It is in this sense that Christ is said to have brought *life and immortality* to light through the gospel.[6]

[1] Rom. viii. 1–10.
[2] Matt. xvi. 25.
[3] 1 Cor. i. 18—ὁ λόγος ὁ τοῦ σταυροῦ.
[4] Cf. 1 John iii. 14–17.
[5] Gal. v. 24 (Revised Version).
[6] 2 Timothy i. 10.

'This gift to men' [I purposely quote a strictly orthodox commentator] 'is not the inculcation of the truth of an endless existence, nor any dogma of the soul's deathless perpetuity, but the revelation of a higher life.'[1]

Life, in the mystical sense indicated, often more specifically 'eternal life', is the very burden of the Fourth Gospel and the Johannine Epistles.[2] 'I am come', says the Johannine Christ, 'that they might have life, and that they might have it more abundantly.'[3] 'He that eateth my flesh and drinketh my blood hath eternal life.'[4] This spiritual sense both of life and of resurrection forms the kernel of the Lazarus story, where it is expressly emphasized against the literalism of Martha. 'Martha saith unto him, I know that he shall rise again in the resurrection at the last day. Jesus said unto her, I am the resurrection and the life: he that believeth in me, though he were dead, yet shall he live: and whosoever liveth and believeth in me shall never die.'[5] So again: 'The hour cometh *and now is*, when the dead shall hear the voice of the Son of God, and they that hear shall live.'[6] This is the same spiritual sense of life and resurrection as an accomplished fact that we have in St. Paul. The dead here are the spiritually dead who are to be quickened or made alive. 'This is life eternal, that they should know thee, the only true God, and Jesus Christ whom thou hast sent.'[7] Similarly in the Epistles: 'God hath given to us eternal life, and this life is in his Son. He that hath the Son hath life.'[8] 'We know that we have passed from death unto life, because we love the brethren. He that loveth not his brother abideth in death.'[9] 'He that loveth not, knoweth

[1] S. D. F. Salmond, *Christian Doctrine of Immortality*, p. 393.

[2] The expression 'eternal life' occurs 'some seventeen times in the Gospel and six times in the Epistles'. Salmond, *op. cit.*, p. 489.

[3] John x. 10.
[4] John vi. 54.
[5] John xi. 24–6.
[6] John v. 25.
[7] John xvii. 3.
[8] 1 John v. 11–12.
[9] 1 John iii. 14.

not God; for God is love.... If we love one another, God abideth in us, and his love is perfected in us.'[1] 'This is the true God, and eternal life.'[2]

The emphatic present tense throughout these passages is evidence sufficient of the writer's meaning. Eternal life is not a state of existence to follow upon physical death, but an all-satisfying present experience of the love of God in Christ. It is, as the theologians say, 'participation in the being of the spiritual Christ'. The fruit of such an experience (to quote St. Paul's list) is 'love, joy, peace'.[3] 'My peace I give unto you', says the Johannine Christ.[4] 'These things have I spoken unto you, that your joy might be full.'[5] 'And ye shall know the truth, and the truth shall make you free.'[6] This is the eternal life in the midst of time which is claimed by the saints as an immediate experience, one which time can neither increase nor diminish, one to which considerations of time are, in fact, indifferent, because we are at rest in the present.

Needless to say, such experience is not the exclusive property of any single faith. Much controversy has raged, for example, round the meaning of the Buddhist Nirvana. The term is ordinarily translated nothingness or annihilation. At his death, we are told, the perfected saint becomes extinct, like the flame of an expiring fire. That appears to be the natural result of the insight he has gained into the root of all evil and the way of deliverance; and the term is so applied by Buddhists themselves. Yet the Buddha himself, when urged by his disciples, expressly declined to answer yea or nay to the question whether the man who has won deliverance will exist or not after death—on the ground that 'this is a matter which does not make for things needful to salvation, nor for that which concerns

[1] 1 John iv. 8-12. [2] 1 John v. 20. [3] Gal. v. 22.
[4] John xiv. 27. [5] John xv. 11. [6] John viii. 32.

a holy life'.[1] What he had taught, he said, was only the cause of suffering and the path which leads to its cessation. The primary reference of the word is, therefore, not to any future event—to what may happen after death—but to the insight on which that ultimate deliverance may be supposed to follow—to the extinction of all the fires of desire and the perfect peace resulting therefrom. Nirvana, in its original intention, is that immediate emancipation from all the passions and cares of life which renunciation brings with it, a state of mind to be attained here and now, the peace which the world can neither give nor take away, and which is the supreme and only blessedness. 'There is no spot, O King, East, South, West, or North, above, below or beyond, where Nirvana is situate, and yet Nirvana is, and he who orders his life aright . . . may realize it, whether he live in Greece, in China, in Alexandria or Kosala.'[2] Apart from the fundamental pessimism of Buddhism, the words of Jesus and those of the Buddha often strikingly resemble one another in their recurring emphasis on rest and peace. And the language of Buddhist hymns is not so different from that of Christian devotion. Take, for instance, these short examples rendered by Mrs. Rhys Davids[3]:—

> Nirvana have I realized, and gazed
> Into the mirror of the Holy Law.
> I, even I, am healèd of my hurt.
> Low is my burden laid, my task is done,
> My heart is wholly set at liberty.
>
> . . . .
>
> Nor is there any bliss greater than peace.
> These things to know, e'en as they really are,
> This is Nirvana, crown of happiness.

Religion is thus, as Hegel has finely said,[4] 'the realm

[1] Mrs. Rhys Davids, *Buddhism*, p. 179.

[2] Mrs. Rhys Davids, *op. cit.*, p. 232.

[3] *op. cit.*, pp. 177, 185

[4] *Werke*, xi, pp. 3–4 (in the opening paragraph of the *Philosophy of Religion*).

where all the riddles of the world are solved, all the contradictions of probing thought are unveiled, and all pangs of feeling cease, the region of eternal truth, of eternal rest. The whole complexity of human relations, activities, enjoyments, everything that man values and esteems, wherein he seeks his happiness, his glory, his pride—all find their final centre in religion, in the thought, the consciousness, the feeling of God. . . . God is known in religion. Religion just means being occupied with this object. In this occupation the spirit casts off all its finitude; in it it finds its satisfaction and perfect freedom. All nations accordingly have looked upon this religious consciousness as their true dignity, as the Sunday of their lives; every care and anxiety, this "bank and shoal of time" itself, vanishes in this aether, in the immediate feeling of devotion or of hope.'

It is, then, on the possibility of such experiences as we have been considering that any valid theory of immortality must be based. Their reality is beyond dispute, whether reached in the apprehension of Truth, through Beauty, or through Goodness. By whatever gate a man may enter, the eternal foundations of the world are there discovered to him, and he knows that in his hold on these realities lies all that is worth striving for, all that is of value in his life. The being of these realities and his own relation to them 'stand sure' beyond the risks of time and change, even the change which we call death. He who has tasted eternal life is not wont to be troubled in heart about the question of his personal survival; for such survival would mean nothing to him, if he were separated from the object in which he has found his true life. His immortality lies for him in his union with the eternal object on which his affections are set, and he seeks no other assurance.

LECTURE VIII

ETERNAL LIFE AND PERSONAL IMMORTALITY

We have still to consider the bearing of Eternal Life, as discussed in the preceding Lecture, upon the question of immortality in the more usual sense of continued existence. For it is undoubtedly the case that emphasis upon these present experiences is frequently associated with a disparagement of the desire for individual survival; and in some quarters the realization of eternal life in this sense is definitely put forward as the religious truth of which the doctrine of personal immortality is a popular distortion.

Spinoza is the greatest of those who appear to regard our present participation in the eternal life of thought as the only kind of immortality we may legitimately contemplate. Yet that was not always his position, and the history of his views, as we are now able to follow it, is instructive. No fewer than three stages are traceable in his printed works. The first is that represented by the *Cogitata Metaphysica*, published in 1663, where he maintains the Cartesian position that the mind is a substance, and therefore in its nature imperishable. '*Liquidissime constat mentes esse immortales.*' This work, however, was appended to an exposition of Descartes's philosophy, drawn up for the use of a rather incompetent pupil—one, too, against whom Spinoza felt it necessary to be on his guard in the expression of his own opinions. It does not, therefore, necessarily represent Spinoza's own position at the date of publication, though it may fairly be taken as giving us the starting-point of his thought. The *Short Treatise on God, on Man, and his Well-being*, on the other hand, unpublished in the author's life-time, and only discovered in a Dutch translation in the middle of last century, gives us the first form in which his characteristic ideas took shape in his own mind. It is in effect a first draft of the *Ethics*, although differing on certain not unimportant points from the final presentation of his system. Intended for a circle of friends in Amsterdam, with whom he had been accustomed to discuss philosophical and religious questions, it is written perhaps with a greater intimacy of feeling. Certainly he uses here the emotional and personal language of religion more frequently than he permits himself to do in the later exposition.

On the question of immortality the *Short Treatise*[1] is particularly interesting as marking a distinct stage in the progress of Spinoza's thought. The soul is no longer for him a substance: he has already formulated his theory of the one Substance, which he calls indifferently nature or God, with its two attributes of extension and thought. The soul is, therefore, now regarded as a mode of the attribute of thought, or, as he here puts it, 'the soul is an idea arising in the *res cogitans* from the existence of something present in nature'. This 'something present in nature' is, of course, the human body: as in the *Ethics*, the soul or mind is the *idea corporis*, the idea or 'objective essence' of the body. 'The soul', he says here,[2] 'as being an idea of the body, derives its first being from the body, for it is only a representation of the body, both as a whole and in its parts, in the thinking thing.' Hence, according to the duration and changes of the body, so must also be the duration and changes of the soul; regarded merely as the idea or representation of the body, the mind must perish with the dissolution of the body whose idea it is. But the mind is not like a dumb picture, the mere

[1] An English translation of the *Short Treatise* with Introduction and Commentary was published in 1910 by Dr. A. Wolf. The Dutch text is printed in the edition of Spinoza's works by Van Vloten and Land.

[2] Bk. II, c. 22 (Wolf, p. 134).

duplicate in thought of the body and its physiological arrangements. The idea of the body, as he puts it in the *Ethics*, is also the idea of itself (*idea ideae*). It is conscious of itself and conscious, therefore, also—or capable at least of becoming conscious—of the whole to which it belongs. Through knowledge, and the love which knowledge breeds, the soul is capable of union with God, and becomes then as eternal as the object of its love. 'For love alone', he says, 'knows no limits; as it increases more and more, so also it grows more excellent, because it is bestowed on an object which is infinite. Hence it, and it alone, can go on increasing for ever.'[1]

Thus the destiny of the soul depends, Spinoza seems to say, on the direction of its affections. In his own formal statement, 'If it [remains] united with the perishable body alone, then it must also perish. But if it becomes united with some other thing, which is unchangeable and abides, then it cannot but be unchangeable also and abide.'[2] A soul with no outlook beyond the body remains, we might say in the language of more recent philosophy, a mere particular, a phenomenon among phenomena that arise and pass away. But the soul which realizes its universal nature conquers time, and lays hold on a life that knows no ending. The phraseology is in many ways a striking anticipation of what we afterwards find in the *Ethics* and in the unfinished treatise *On the Improvement of the Understanding*. But in the *Short Treatise* Spinoza still uses the old terminology. He speaks of 'the immortality of the soul' and devotes a special chapter to the proof, preparing the way for it by several forward references in the earlier stages of his argument. He appears to have frankly in mind an individual immortality; and as he does not yet use the terms eternal and eternity in the technical sense, as defined in the

[1] Bk. II, c. 14. [2] Bk. II, c. 23.

Ethics, immortality appears to be used in the popular sense of unending duration.

It is more than doubtful whether this position is maintained in the much-discussed series of propositions at the close of the *Ethics* (v. 21–40), in which Spinoza expounds what he means by the *pars aeterna nostri*; for there he lays it down at the outset that imagination and memory are entirely dependent on bodily conditions. 'The mind cannot imagine anything nor remember things past, except while the body endures.' Nevertheless, he proceeds, 'the human mind cannot be absolutely destroyed with the body, but something of it remains which is eternal.'[1] The word immortality, however, has disappeared from the *Ethics*[2], and we are expressly reminded in the scholium to this proposition that 'eternity cannot be defined in terms of time nor can it have any relation to time'. We have left, in short, all individual facts behind us, including individual persons. It is the mind constituted by understanding, conceiving the system of eternal or necessary truth and reality, that is eternal, and it alone.[3] 'The mind', he says again, 'is eternal in so far as it conceives things under the form of eternity,'[4] that is to say, 'as contained in God, and following from the necessity of the divine nature'.[5] If everywhere for 'eternal' we read 'necessary', and if at the same time we keep in view Spinoza's warning that mind, in the sense in which he is now speaking of it, had no beginning but must be thought of as necessarily constituted by this knowledge and eternally possessing the blessedness which belongs to it,[6] the conclusion is irresistible, that what he is speaking of is not any individual self, but either an impersonal system

[1] v. 23. [2] It reappears, however, in the scholium to v. 41.

[3] As the context shows: '*Mentis enim oculi, quibus res videt observatque, sunt ipsae demonstrationes.*' v. 23.

[4] v. 31, Sch. [5] v. 29, Sch. [6] v. 33.

of thought, or, if a self is involved as an eternal thinker of the systematic whole, it must be of the pattern of Aristotle's God, who, also, according to that philosopher, realizes a perfect blessedness in the exercise of his self-contemplation. The finite individual may, indeed, during life place himself at this universal standpoint and taste this eternal joy; and while he does so, his love, in Spinoza's mystical phrase, is part of the infinite love wherewith God loves himself;[1] but everything that characterizes him as a finite individual vanishes with the body which is the symbol of his finitude. The resemblance between Spinoza's 'eternal part' of the mind and Aristotle's doctrine of the Active Reason is too striking to need insisting on. And Spinoza's substitution of the eternal life of thought, which can be lived here and now, for immortality in the usual sense of a continued personal existence, recalls what was said in the second lecture of a similar sense of the term in Plato and Aristotle. To Plato, indeed, and his conception of the eternal reality of the Ideas, we may trace the origin of this use of the term, although Plato himself did not regard the enjoyment of eternal life in this sense as ruling out the possibility of personal immortality, or as a substitute for it.

Among contemporary thinkers, Professor Bosanquet, although himself perhaps the most eminent representative in this country of an idealistic or spiritual philosophy, has uniformly adopted a negative attitude towards personal immortality. It forms part of his general polemic against what he calls, somewhat contemptuously, 'transcendent theism or polytheism and the persistent finite individual subject';[2] and he frequently connects the discussion with the distinction on which he lays so much stress between the moralistic and the properly religious attitude of mind

[1] v. 36.

[2] *Meeting of Extremes in Contemporary Philosophy*, Preface.

towards the universe.[1] We have already recognized the justice of this distinction and the necessity of transcending the purely moralistic attitude, if a satisfactory doctrine of immortality is to be reached.[2] At the standpoint of 'individualistic morality', the situation resolves itself into an infinite progress of approximation to a perfection which can never be realized; and precisely the endlessness of the process was converted by Kant into an argument for the immortality of the soul. The inflexible command of reason (so he states the argument in the second Postulate of the Practical Reason) is the perfect accordance of the will with the moral law. But in a being, sensitive as well as rational, this conformity is never more than partial. Nevertheless, whatever the Imperative demands must be possible; if a holy will is not possible in man as a present achievement, it must be realizable, under the form of an endless progress or continual approximation to the idea of holiness. In this way the ethical Imperative guarantees to us an infinite time in which to work out its behest: the immortality of the individual is bound up with the moral law as a necessary condition of its fulfilment. To this strained and unconvincing argument Professor Bosanquet effectively opposes the religious experience in which the individual, recognizing once for all the impotence of his finite striving, surrendering all claims to goodness on his own account, 'recognizes [in the same act] his unity with the divine goodness by faith, and so shares at once the perfection which, as finite, he could not win by any striving'.[3] This, as he often tells us, is the meaning of

[1] e.g. *Value and Destiny of the Individual*, Lecture V. Quite recently he wrote: 'I insist on the antithesis—the opposition of the purely moralistic or ethical and the profoundly religious attitude—because I believe that it is more and more emerging as the dividing line and divergent aspiration of modern modes of thought' (*Mind*, N. S., vol. 30, p. 98).

[2] Cf. pp. 134-5 *supra*.

[3] In the Symposium reprinted in the volume *Life and Finite Individuality*, p. 187. The recognition by the individual of his 'unity with the

justification by faith—and faith in this sense is the fruitful parent of works (being, of course, 'dead' without them). Religion, that is to say, includes morality within itself, but it gives, in addition, the all-important sense of security and peace, through the individual's identification of himself with a divine world-order in which the supremacy of the good is for ever achieved. This, 'the only perfection possible for a finite individual, we can have here and now, and it is certain and fulfils, through faith and its implication for the will, our utmost conation'.[1] So Professor Bosanquet concludes, and he proceeds to dismiss the idea of a future life as uncalled for, and as founded on the religiously false idea of the conservation of the finite as finite in a hopeless struggle endlessly prolonged.

But this antithesis is surely unfairly pressed both by Professor Bosanquet and by others; and, so far as our present argument is concerned, it appears to be not quite fairly stated. Individualistic moralism, as represented by the Kantian argument, certainly prescribes to man a hopeless task. What guarantee is there, indeed, that the progress will be uniformly in an upward direction? We have already seen the hopelessness of salvation by works in the treadmill operation of Karma. Release from the endlessly revolving wheel came only through some metaphysical or religious insight, some access of saving knowledge. But it is the presupposition of the argument we are at present considering, that the individual has here and now realized his rootedness in the eternal. And because there is no satisfaction in the unending progress of the

divine goodness' is elsewhere described as 'his identification by faith with the greatness of the universe' (*Value and Destiny*, p. xxxii). So again, in *The Meeting of Extremes*: 'We are one with the whole by faith and not in works. Here our inadequacy is done away. This is the very meaning of "saving experiences". We throw ourselves upon the grace of the universe and find in oneness with it an adequacy which is self-contradictory for us as finite agents' (p. 173).

[1] *Life and Finite Individuality*, p. 191.

unsupported finite, it does not follow that the attainment of religious insight in the present life involves the surrender of any hope of a personal life beyond. Why should not the apprehension of the eternal rather carry with it the gift of further life and a fuller fruition? This seemed to be the sense of Spinoza's argument in the *Short Treatise.* It is doubtless true that 'endless duration makes good no better nor white any whiter';[1] but Aristotle was speaking of abstract qualities or essences, which are by definition eternally the same, not of a living experience of which duration is an intrinsic characteristic, and which, in view of its infinite object, can grow indefinitely in richness and depth and comprehensiveness. So St. Paul prays for the Ephesians that they, 'being rooted and grounded in love, may be able to comprehend with all saints what is the breadth, and length, and depth, and height; and to know the love of Christ, which passeth knowledge, that [they may] be filled with all the fulness of God'.[2] Are we to suppose that the capacities of our nature for such a comprehension can reach their limit in the intermittent glimpses of our earthly pilgrimage? Advance in such an intercourse has nothing of the exhausting suggestion of the endless progress, for each moment has its own eternity; there is no aimless heaping up of merit, but an ever deeper appreciation of what, in principle, we already enjoy—'the depth of the riches both of the wisdom and knowledge of God'.[3] St. Paul at least believed fervently in a real advance in such experience: 'I count not myself yet to have apprehended: but one thing I do, forgetting the things which are behind, and stretching forward to the things which are before, I press on toward the goal unto the prize of the high calling of God in Christ Jesus.'[4] Throughout the New Testament, accordingly, even in the

[1] *Nic. Eth.*, Bk. I, c. 6. [2] Eph. iii. 18–19. [3] Rom. xi. 33.
[4] Phil. iii. 13.

passages which most clearly treat 'eternal life' as realized here and now, the present experience is never taken as foreclosing the possibility of a future life, but always rather as a foretaste, as an assurance, indeed, of a fuller realization hereafter. The present is linked with the future in almost every passage, and that would seem to be the natural line of inference. 'The water that I shall give him shall become in him a well of water springing up unto eternal life.'[1]

This was in fact historically the natural sequence of thought, as we saw at the very outset of our survey. It was through the present experience of individual communion with God that the Jews were led to a belief in immortality in any real sense; and again, in Greece, it was participation in the eternal life of the god, as an actual experience, which led directly to theories of the heavenly origin and heavenly destiny of the soul.

But Professor Bosanquet's negative attitude on this question is but a part of his whole treatment of the finite individual. His argument against the continued existence of the individual seems to me equally valid against its existence now. As a matter of fact, in reading Professor Bosanquet or Mr. Bradley, we frequently find ourselves wondering why, on their principles, there should be finite centres of experience at all, so uniformly disparaging is the tone adopted towards them. Professor Bosanquet does tell us that 'there can be no infinity without finiteness', no perfection without imperfection. All that exists is finite, and it is only in this finite world that 'reality' can be said to exist or 'appear'.[2] Yet both writers constantly speak of such separate existence as a defect, or even as a species of illusion. 'The plurality of souls in the Absolute', says Mr. Bradley, 'is appearance, and their existence is not genuine. . . . To gain consistency and

[1] John iv. 14.

[2] *Value and Destiny*, pp. 14-15.

truth, it must be merged, and re-composed in a result in which its specialty must vanish.'[1] 'Taken together in the whole,' he says accordingly, 'appearances, as such, cease.'[2] 'In the Absolute' (to quote his striking phrase) 'the individual attains the complete gift and dissipation of his personality', in which 'he, as such, must vanish'.[3] But I have contended on various occasions[4] that this view involves a complete misreading of the function of individuation in the universe. Individuation is the very method, it may be said, of creation: without it there would be no finite world at all. And the existence of a finite world is not to be thought of as something that just happens to the Absolute, or develops itself within the Absolute only to be 'suppressed' again, 'merged' or 'absorbed'. On the contrary, the finite world is part of the inherent structure of reality. It is a process into which God pours his own life and receives it again with interest. And individuation is the method of the process, an individuation growing in distinctness and independence till it culminates in the self-conscious spirit of man, who, just because he has his own *locus* of existence, can enter into communion with his fellows and with his creative Source. 'We know that the universe is in itself the realization of values', says Professor Bosanquet,[5] and he urges that this should be sufficient for us. But there are no values apart from their realization, that is, apart from consciousness. Spirits are the bearers, the home, of values, so far as the finite world is concerned; and they may well be said, therefore, to constitute for a Divine Spirit the supreme values of that world. It seems strangely inconsistent for Professor Bosanquet to speak, as he does, of the world as 'the vale of soul-making'—to say that 'the moulding of souls is the main work of the

[1] *Appearance and Reality*, pp. 304–6.
[2] *Ibid.*, p. 511.
[3] *Ibid.*, p. 419.
[4] Cf. *The Idea of God*, Lectures XIV and XV *passim*.
[5] *Life and Finite Individuality*, p. 191.

universe as finite'—and yet to insist so strongly on the evanescence of the product. But it is due to the fact that his universe consists, not of God and man, but of a non-personal Absolute and its appearances—an Absolute which uses finite individuals as forms or modes of its self-expression, without conferring upon them any real life of their own. Hence it seems to him 'more natural to suppose that our brief existence is the temporal appearance of some character of the whole. . . . For what appears as a passage in time, the Absolute has need to express itself through us as very subordinate units. . . . While we serve as units, to speak the language of appearance, the Absolute lives in us a little, and for a little time; when its life demands our existence no longer, we yet blend with it as the pervading features or characters, which we were needed for a passing moment to emphasize.'[1]

How far such a conception falls short of the idea of spiritual communion! Professor Bosanquet speaks from time to time of 'a universal mind' and 'a universal experience'; but more frequently his expressions leave us in doubt whether the Absolute really possesses the spiritual unity which would enable it to enjoy the process of its own experience. Kaleidoscopic changes apparently go on within it; but it is difficult to say for whom, seeing that 'the Absolute', he tells us, 'is never itself a subject or a predicate—or a spectator or a knower. It is always the whole and it cannot be a part of itself, though divisions and conditions have relative being within it.'[2] It is 'the totality of things as a totality', 'rather the theatre of good and evil than good or evil in itself', or, again, 'the whole considered as a perfection in which the antagonism of good and evil is unnoted'.[3] 'The general form of the Absolute', he says elsewhere,[4] is 'the transmutation and rearrangement of

[1] *Life and Finite Individuality*, pp. 101-2. [2] *Ibid.*, p. 194.
[3] *Value and Destiny*, pp. 250-1. [4] *Individuality and Value*, p. 373.

particular experiences, and also of the contents of particular finite minds, by inclusion in a completed whole of experience'. But the whole, just as such, seems to be little better than an empty space in which everything happens.

When Mr. Bradley's *Appearance and Reality* was published, nearly thirty years ago, I ventured to criticize[1] his celebrated description of the Absolute as 'neither personal nor moral nor beautiful nor true', and to point out the inevitable effect upon the mind of this cluster of negations. Either the Absolute will be regarded, I said, as a mere Unknowable with which we have no concern, or the denial of the attributes in question—personality, morality, beauty, and truth—will be taken to mean that it is a unity indifferent to these higher aspects of experience. 'Both religion and the higher poetry', I said, 'just because they give up the pretence of an impossible exactitude, carry us, I cannot doubt, nearer to the meaning of the world than the formulae of an abstract metaphysic.' It has been, therefore, a very genuine satisfaction to me to find Mr. Bradley himself returning to the subject after many years in a more positive mood—with a desire, as he expresses it, 'to lay a different emphasis upon some aspects of the question'. In these later essays, while still maintaining his general metaphysical position, he acknowledges that an obstinate demand for theoretic consistency may easily defeat its own object, and assures us that 'the ideas which best express our highest religious needs and their satisfaction must certainly be true', in the sense of possessing the practical truth that matters.[2]

One characteristic of the great experiences considered

[1] In two articles on 'A New Theory of the Absolute', published in the *Contemporary Review* and since reprinted in *Man's Place in the Cosmos*.

[2] *Essays on Truth and Reality*, p. 431. 'I find myself', he adds, 'now taking more and more as literal fact what I used in my youth to admire and love as poetry' (468 n.).

in the previous lecture may be an important clue to us in our present inquiry—I mean the complete objectivity of our attitude, our complete absorption in the object. The selfishness of the desire for immortality is one of the commonest charges brought against those who plead for it. So far from being a religious doctrine or an important adjunct to religious faith, it betokens in reality, it is urged, an essentially irreligious frame of mind. The very note of religion is self-surrender, self-forgetfulness, absorption in others, losing our merely personal life to find it in larger ends and common sacrifices; whereas the stickler for immortality seems to be either unhealthily preoccupied with his personal fortunes in the world to come, or inclined to make his individual survival a test case by which to determine the justice or injustice of the cosmic arrangements. But a doctrine of immortality conceived in religious terms and maintained on religious grounds entirely escapes such censure; for the type of experience to which it points, so far from exhibiting preoccupation with self, is of a kind in which explicit consciousness of self may be said to disappear in the absorbing consciousness of the object. The lover has no eyes but for his mistress, no thoughts but of her: the deeper and the purer his passion, the more is this the case. So it is with the love of God. The joys of heaven for the genuinely religious man (it must in justice be said) are not conceived as extraneous rewards conferred on him for his faithfulness to the divine cause during life. They are thought of as a continuation and intensification of the communion he has already enjoyed. It is the all-satisfying vision of God himself in which the rapture of the saints consists, and such rapture excludes all lesser thoughts. So Dante describes the Beatific Vision:

> Così la mente mia, tutta sospesa,
> mirava fissa, immobile ed attenta,
> e sempre del mirar faceasi accesa.

A quella luce cotal si diventa,
che volgersi da lei per altro aspetto
è impossibil che mai si consenta.[1]

In any experience of intense fruition there is a similar absorption of the whole mind and being in the object, the same absence of reflective preoccupation with the self or enjoying subject. The experience may be that of utter delight in the beauty of natural objects or of some work of art, or it may be the passion of the intellect as a tangled mass of facts falls at last into order and symmetry. In some supreme revelations of beauty and sublimity the discursive reason seems for the time suspended in its function, as in the vision described by Wordsworth in the First Book of *The Excursion*:

His spirit drank
The spectacle: sensation, soul and form
All melted into him; they swallowed up
His animal being; in them did he live,
And by them did he live, they were his life.
In such access of mind, in such high hour
Of visitation from the living God,
Thought was not; in enjoyment it expired.

Such experiences bring us to the verge of mysticism. But another lesson we may learn from them is that they lend no countenance to the idea sometimes supposed to be involved in mysticism, that in such supreme communion the distinction between subject and object disappears, that the two are actually fused or commingled, and in particular that the religious goal of the finite spirit is, in such an experience, to yield up its individual being and be merged in the divine essence. This is undoubtedly the aspiration of some mystics. I have quoted elsewhere the words of Labadie, the French Pietist. 'I surrender my soul heartily

[1] *Paradiso*, xxxiii. 97–104. 'Thus all absorbèd did my mind gaze, fixed, immovable, intent, and ever enkindled by its gazing. Such doth the spirit become in presence of that light, it never can consent to turn from it to regard aught else, for the good which is the object of the will is therein wholly gathered.'

to God', he wrote in his last will and testament, 'giving it back like a drop of water to its source . . . praying God, my origin and ocean, that He will take me unto himself and engulf me eternally in the divine abyss of his Being.' The raindrop and the ocean is a favourite metaphor, and there are many others, all expressing the same idea of physical 'engulfment' or absorption. But material metaphors are quite inapplicable to the relation of an intelligence to the object of its knowledge or its love. The experiences we have been considering show us that absorption of mind and heart in an object does not mean the disappearance of the knowing and feeling subject by its being absorbed into the substance of that which it contemplates. So far from implying any such thing, absorption in the object, if we consider it as a real experience, means the intensest concentration of the subject mind and its fullest fruition. I believe that in the literature of mysticism there is often an unobserved transition from absorption in the sense of concentration upon an object to absorption in the sense of being sucked under, as it were, and physically incorporated in the being of the object. The higher mysticism, I should judge, rests upon the first sense; but with less speculative and less truly religious minds the material metaphor becomes more and more dominant. We never know how deep our materialism goes.

The idea of reabsorption in God seems to rest partly on the conception of individual soul-substances being reincorporated in the parent mass from which they had been temporarily severed. But this is to think of the creation of souls as a process of fission, a mode of reproduction such as takes place in low organisms. If we reflect that the reality of any finite spirit is the formed mind and will which is the result of the long moulding process, and that this result is something absolutely new and unique in the universe, a creation in the most literal sense, then it

s plain that the so-called reabsorption of the individual
nto his divine source does not mean that anything is
ictually refunded into the Divine Being, to enrich it, or
o be used afresh for further creations. It means simply
he disappearance of the personality in question. And to
'epresent this as, in each case, the goal and consummation
of the creative process, seems little less than contradictory
—unless, indeed, we secretly suppose that the divine
'esources could not equip, or could not keep in mind,
ı really infinite world of spirits, so that they have to die,
ıs their turn comes, to make room for others who take
heir place. It was in such a spirit that the Stoics discussed
he difficulty: 'If souls survive, how can the air hold them
'rom all eternity?' And they came to the conclusion
:hat, just as the bodies of generation after generation are
:ommitted to the dust and resolved into the elements, so,
:ven if they should survive for a time, souls are before
ong transmuted into air and thus resumed into the seminal
orinciple of the universe.[1] But, just as the goods of the
spirit are not lessened by being shared, but rather increased,
so there is no consumption of material in the making of
souls, no exhaustion of the resources of the universe.
The capacities of self-conscious experience, as they emerge
into being in the appropriate circumstances—the personalities thus built up, with the powers of appreciation
ınd enjoyment involved—are a sheer enrichment of the
world, an enrichment which, so to speak, costs nothing.
They are in truth, as I have already argued,[2] creations, each
fresh and unique, not so much old material worked up;
ınd therefore there is, in principle, no limit to the creative
process, no reason why the Power from whom they draw
:heir existence should intervene to dissolve the personalities
:hus called into being.

[1] Cf. Marcus Aurelius, *Meditation*, Bk. IV. 21.
[2] Cf. pp. 128–9, *supra*.

M 2

The sense of contradiction in that supposition reache a curious climax in the closing lines of George Eliot' poem *The Legend of Jubal*, where she makes Jubal fad away into forgetfulness,

> Quitting mortality, a quenched sun-wave,
> The All-creating Presence for his grave.

Plato has a nobler idea of what befits a Creator. In th strange medley of phantasy and wisdom which he ha bequeathed to us in the *Timaeus*, he makes the Creato thus address the spirits he has called into being. A having come into being, he tells them, they possess n inherent eternity. 'All that is bound may be dissolved but only an evil being would wish to dissolve that which is harmonious and happy. In my will ye have a greate and a mightier bond than that which bound you at th time of creation'.[1] But George Eliot's phrase possesses a least this merit: the word 'grave' does not suggest eithe that the All-creating Presence recovers anything of th nature of soul-material by the quenching of Jubal's per sonality, or that Jubal himself is somehow indemnified b the mode of his disappearance, as if it were a species o apotheosis in which he became part of a larger life. He is simply 'quenched': his light is put out, and God himsel is poorer thereby. I think it is important to realize the completely illusory character of all vague talk about merging and reabsorption. When Schleiermacher tries to comfort the mourning widow by telling her that 'melt-ing away into the great All' should be thought of as 'a merging not into death but into life, and that the highest life', his words have no meaning unless the living self survives to realize the fruition of the union. When he goes on to say that this merging is 'what we all strive after in this life, only that we never reach it, viz. to live

[1] *Timaeus*, 41.

imply in the Divine whole to which we belong, and to ut away from us the pretension to set up for ourselves', ie lets us see quite clearly the underlying confusion etween the conscious identification of our private will vith the divine will and the cessation of the individual onsciousness altogether.[1]

Nevertheless some, even of those who contend most strenuously for a continuance of personal life beyond he grave, appear still to contemplate something of the iature of absorption as the final consummation. No nore strenuous, at times one might even say more ntemperate, advocate of personal immortality could be iamed than Tennyson. In a familiar passage he rejects he idea of absorption:

> That each, who seems a separate whole,
> Should move his rounds, and fusing all
> The skirts of self again, should fall
> Re-merging in the general Soul,
>
> Is faith as vague as all unsweet:
> Eternal form shall still divide
> The eternal soul from all beside;
> And I shall know him when we meet.

Yet the section of 'In Memoriam'[2] which opens with these stanzas concludes by abating the claim to a literal eternity of the individual, and states love's minimum in other terms. Love

> seeks at least
>
> Upon the last and sharpest height
> Before the spirits fade away,
> Some landing-place, to clasp and say,
> 'Farewell! We lose ourselves in light.'

And the same idea of a final consummation is perhaps suggested in the lines with which the poem ends—

> Until we close with all we loved,
> And all we flow from, soul in soul.

[1] See Martineau's *Study of Religion*, ii. 359.

[2] Section XLVII.

From the *Memoir* we gather that the idea of an ultimate absorption into the divine, after many a passage 'from death to death, through life and life',[1] was not repugnant to him, as that of an immediate absorption undoubtedly was. 'If the absorption into the divine in the after-life be the creed of some, let them at all events allow us many existences of individuality before this absorption; since this short-lived individuality seems to be but too short a preparation for so mighty a union'.[2]

This view has been recently put forward dogmatically by Troeltsch, one of the most eminent contemporary theologians of Germany.[3] Maintaining what he calls a personalistic eschatology—teaching, that is to say, a further life, or lives, involving a continuous process of moral purification and an ever-increasing identification of the human will with the divine—he yet holds that the final end of the whole ethical process must be 'the union of the creature with God' (Gotteinigung der Creatur), his 'submergence' (Wiederuntergehen) in the divine life. 'The actual end would thus be the complete unity of will with the divine will eventually achieved in this further development after death and a confluence of the finite wills in love, so that perfected love, the complete disappearance of the perfected individuals, the yielding up of the personality to the divine life would be the final end.' The word used to describe the fate of the individual is very strong—Verzehrung, a consuming as by fire, a devouring which leaves no remnant, a total dissipation. 'And the value of the whole process [he continues] would be the blessedness of the ethico-personal values thus laboriously achieved, which reach their culmination

[1] *De Profundis*. [2] *Memoir*, i. 319.

[3] The quotations which follow are from an article on Eschatology in Schiele's Encyclopaedia, *Die Religion in Geschichte und Gegenwart*, vol. ii. 622-31. I owe the reference to Professor H. R. Mackintosh.

precisely in the final moment. The highest or perfect blessedness would be the last moment, and it would kill the finite being, inasmuch as it raises it above itself and thereby annihilates it.' So in the old mythology Semele perished in the embrace of Zeus: but that was recognized as a catastrophe, not a consummation—death for the mortal and grief for the god. Such a culmination of a spiritual process is self-contradictory and indeed unmeaning. Underlying Troeltsch's phraseology there seems to be the material metaphor of pouring or transfusing the divine essence into the individual soul as into a finite vessel, which at a given point in the process is inevitably shivered to pieces by the expanding content. But a process of growth in knowledge and spiritual communion cannot be so conceived, and the catastrophic conclusion is no more appropriate at the end of many lives than at the end of one. In Troeltsch's case, its supposed necessity seems to be based mainly on the horror with which the idea of a never-ending existence inspires him: the thought, he says, is 'erschreckend und erschütternd'. But that, again, is because the future life takes for him the form of an infinite progress in moral attainment rather than the continuous enjoyment of an ever-present good. The paralysing idea of the unending process produces, accordingly, what we know to be its inevitable effect on the imagination; and, simply to escape from the intolerableness of the situation, we are impelled to give the process *some* ultimate goal or consummation, even should it be of this catastrophic description. But it belongs to the very nature of the eternal values to deliver us from this nightmare of the imagination. Art, as Schopenhauer told us, is everywhere at its goal, and so is religion.

LECTURE IX

SOME ARGUMENTS REVIEWED

WE have reviewed in the course of these lectures a number of specific arguments for immortality, or, as they used to be often more ambitiously called, proofs. But the more ambitious they were, the less convincing, I am afraid, we found them. It is needless at this stage to go back upon them in detail. The typical metaphysical argument was that from the unity and simplicity of the soul. It has a place of honour in the forefront of Bishop Butler's treatise, and it still appears in Roman Catholic manuals. As I argued at length, it is based on a false analogy and entirely misconceives the nature of the unity and identity which really characterize the self. It cannot, therefore, throw any light on its future destiny, much less furnish us with a demonstration of its endless existence. With the exception of Dr. McTaggart, there are, I think, few philosophers at the present day who put their trust in metaphysical arguments to prove the intrinsic or necessary immortality of the soul. In his hands, the doctrine of such eternal self-subsistent selves is found to exclude the existence of God as an Absolute Spirit on whom they depend; for each of these selves, though appearing to develop in time, is really perfect, a god in his own right. If, on the other hand, with the theologians, we suppose the selves to be created beings, we make both their present and their future existence dependent on the divine will; and any conclusion at which we may arrive as to the future ought not to differ in principle from Lotze's 'general idealistic conviction that every created thing will continue, if, and so long as, its continuance belongs to the meaning of the world.' The truth is, as Kant sarcastically observes after his destructive criticism of this very argument from substantiality to immortality, 'the merely speculative proof has never had any influence upon the common reason of men. It stands upon the point of a hair, so that even the schools have been able to preserve it from falling only by incessantly discussing it and spinning it like a top.' He points us on, therefore, to the Practical Reason as the only sphere in which we may hope to reach assurance.

But before passing altogether from the metaphysical arguments, based more or less on the idea of the substantiality of the soul, it may not be amiss to recall the real meaning, or underlying motive, of the assertion that the soul or mind is a substance. It is a sound canon of interpretation that the best way to arrive at the true meaning of the formulae of an ecclesiastical creed is to consider the heresies they were intended to deny. The same principle holds good in the case of philosophical doctrines; and if we apply this test, it is obvious that the motive prompting the assertion of the soul's substantiality was the wish to deny that the conscious life is, so to speak, merely an attribute, or, in the more usual phrase, only a function of body—body alone possessing the kind of permanent reality usually associated with the term substance. In the fourth and fifth of these lectures, on Mind and Body, I adversely criticized the animistic idea of soul and body as two separate interacting substances, and defended, in its general outline, the Aristotelian conception of the soul as the entelechy or 'function' of the body. But by function—if we are to use the term—Aristotle understood the end or purpose for which the body exists; and it was the soul, he said, to which we should apply in a pre-eminent sense the predicates 'unity' and 'reality'. The word function is used, however, in materialistic arguments with a totally different emphasis, to suggest that states of consciousness are simply the transient results or accompaniments of certain bodily processes which it is as unreasonable to suppose surviving the organism as to suppose the odour of a rose surviving when the rose itself has perished. This is evidently to deny that there is any such unity as the soul at all. This type of materialistic argument appears already as a current doctrine in the *Phaedo*, where Simmias the Theban, a disciple of the later Pythagorean school, compares the relation of body and soul to that of the lyre and the tune played upon it. To assert the immortality of the soul is, according to the figure, as if we attributed to the tune a substantive existence of its own, which would enable it to survive when the lyre was broken and the strings cut or snapped. Plato criticizes this theory and his answer is, in essence, to point out that the soul does exhibit a real unity and activity which makes the analogy of the lyre and the tune inapplicable. Plato refers to the way in which the soul takes command of the body, opposing the passions and 'leading all the elements of which she is said to consist'.[1] It is the reality of the self as an organized and centrally active unity of this description which people mean to assert when they describe the mind as a substance. They mean to deny the conception of the mind as no more than detached states of consciousness floating off from the body at intervals, or even in a continuous stream. I laid great stress, in the fifth lecture, on this centrality and organized unity as the true reality of the spiritual self, which the unfortunate term substance had been used to indicate. In looking since then into Mill's *Essays on Religion*, I have been pleased to find the same view strongly stated there. 'We need not be de-

[1] *Phaedo*, 86.

terred', he says,[1] 'by any metaphysical difficulties about a thinking substance' in the traditional sense of the term; 'wherever there is a series of thoughts connected together by memories, that constitutes a thinking substance' in the practical application of the words. Mill was notoriously in revolt against the old terminology, yet he emphatically repudiates the idea of mind as a mere retainer of matter. In fact he does not hesitate to describe mind as 'the only substantive reality',[2] and to reject any conclusions as to its fate drawn from the analogy of material objects. This does not, of course, imply, either for Mill or for us, that the soul is necessarily or inherently immortal, but only that the kind of reality which belongs to it, as we know it in the present life, is such that the hypothesis of its survival is one which may be reasonably entertained and discussed on its merits.

With this reminder we may pass to the moral arguments, and there, as we shall presently see, much discrimination is necessary if the reasoning is to be presented in a form that can be accepted as ultimately valid. The moral argument for a future life is bound up with the conception of the universe as a moral order. It may be said to start, as we see in Butler, from the rudimentary moral order actually observable in the natural course of things, virtue and vice having each their natural consequences, the one making on the whole for stability, co-operation and happiness, and the other tending in the long run to the opposite results. In such linkage of consequences we perceive, as Butler says, 'somewhat moral in the essential constitution of things'.[3] In what concerns the conduct of human life these natural sanctions may be taken, he says, as 'a declaration, in some degree of present effect, from Him who is supreme in nature, which side he is of, or what

[1] *Three Essays on Religion*, p. 200. [2] *Ibid.*, p. 203.
[3] *Analogy*, Part I, c. 3.

part he takes—a declaration for virtue and against vice.' In Matthew Arnold's vaguer phrase, they are evidence of 'an enduring power, not ourselves, which makes for righteousness.' The instinct of self-preservation prompts a similar discrimination against certain actions in the penal codes of human societies. But, as both natural and civil sanctions operate imperfectly in the present world, belief in the moral constitution of the universe carries with it (so the argument proceeds) the promise of a more perfect vindication of virtue and a more effective punishment of vice, from which no criminal may hope to escape. The future world thus comes to be conceived as primarily a system of rewards and punishments which shall satisfy our sense of justice. It was in this way, as we have seen, that, under the influence of a developing moral sense, the colourless primitive theories of continuance were transformed into theories of retribution; and, as I pointed out at the time, although retribution, or the rendering to a man according to his deeds, undoubtedly covers rewards as well as punishments, the term is predominantly associated with punishment, and punishment has all along figured most prominently in popular theories of the future life. Even Butler's chapter on the subject is significantly headed 'Of the government of God by rewards and punishments, and particularly of the latter.'

This concentration of the mind on punishment has had many demoralizing results. Men's views about punishment are an index of their own advance in moral insight and in humane manners. The now discredited *lex talionis*, the savage precept of an eye for an eye, a tooth for a tooth, was itself in its origin a humanitarian reform. By fixing a definite legal penalty for definite offences, it sought to set limits to the unrestrained fury of private revenge; its aim was, indeed, to supersede private revenge altogether by vesting the punishment of crime in the community as such.

But the vindictive theory of punishment for punishment's sake obviously persists in these legalized penalties; and although the scale of penalties tended in the course of ages to become more rational and more humane, the theory of punishment as an act of retributive justice called for by the nature of things, quite irrespective of its effects upon the criminal or as a deterrent to others, dominated ethics and jurisprudence till comparatively recent times, and is probably not without defenders at the present day. But there is, at any rate, a growing consciousness among thoughtful people, and especially, I should say, among those who have practically to do with the administration of the law, that punishment is not an end in itself; it can be rationally defended only so far as it seeks to reform the criminal or, failing that, to secure the community against the repetition of that particular kind of crime.

Such has been the general line of advance in regard to earthly punishments. But in speculating upon the punishments of a future life, man has often seemed to fall back on the primitive instinct of revenge, and even to indulge by proxy ancestral lusts of cruelty in piling up the physical torments of the damned. The theoretical basis of Karma as well as of the Orphic teaching is doubtless compensation rigidly exact; the wrongdoer suffers in another life the very wrong he had inflicted in this. Yet the debt had been already paid, with interest accumulated a thousandfold, by ages of agony in the multitudinous hells provided by Eastern imagination for the intermediate state. The horrors of the Orphic hell, peopled with fabulous monsters, are caricatured by Aristophanes. Plato himself, in the Vision of Er, conjures up wild flaming figures who seize upon the incurable sinners as they endeavour to escape, bind them hand and foot, flay them with scourges, drag them by the wayside and card them like wool upon thorn-bushes.[1] So

[1] *Republic*, 615–16.

we can still see represented on Etruscan tombs the hideous figure of Charun, with his attendant demons and furies, a figure with flaming eyes and savage aspect, with the ears and often the tusks of a brute, carrying in his hands a hammer and an instrument of torture.[1] The mediaeval hell, with its cunningly devised varieties of torture and attendant demons who gloat over their infliction, does not stand behind such models. But it was reserved for Jonathan Edwards to portray God himself as carrying through the work of the demons, more savage than an infuriated beast. 'An angry wild beast, if stirred up, will easily tear such an one as thou art to pieces. What canst thou do in the hands of God? . . . If you cry to God to pity you, he will only tread you under foot. He will crush you under his feet without mercy; he will crush out your blood and make it fly, and it shall be sprinkled on his garments so as to stain all his raiment.'[2] 'There was such a breathing of distress and weeping', a contemporary says, 'that the preacher was obliged to speak to the people, and desire silence that he might be heard.' When we reflect upon the torture of apprehension inflicted through the centuries, precisely on the most sensitive natures, by such ideas of God and his dealings with his creatures, we can but echo the Lucretian words—

Tantum religio potuit suadere malorum.

Naturally such pictures of the after-life have played in every age and country into the hands of priestcraft and superstition, so that the Epicurean creed which made death the end of all seemed to the Roman poet by comparison like daylight and pure air after the senseless terrors of the night.

[1] Cf. Dennis, *Cities and Cemeteries of Etruria*, ii. 191.

[2] *Works*, vol. vii, pp. 460–3, in a sermon on 'Sinners in the hands of an angry God'.

It is not along the path of punishment, I am convinced, that we shall reach a reasonable theory of a future life. We can hardly expect to vindicate the necessity of an after-life simply as a security for the punishment of the wicked. Undoubtedly the natural desire is strong to see the oppressor, the cruel and the heartless, suffer something of what they have inflicted upon others; and when they successfully elude earthly justice, there is satisfaction in the thought of Minos, or Rhadamanthus, who will bring them to account.[1] Inhuman cruelty may so exasperate our feelings that they seem to contain nothing but an absorbing passion for revenge. But normally, I am inclined to think, there is wrapped up in the feeling, as its ethical core, the idea that through the suffering the criminal will be brought to look at things from another standpoint and thereby realize the enormity of his own conduct. Purgatorial pain, however, as an element in the great process of the making of souls, stands on quite a different footing from the retributive punishment which we are at present considering; and, therefore, we may pass to the parallel case of rewards, similarly regarded as demanded by justice or involved in the conception of moral government.

We need not waste time over those who regard morality as entirely a matter of positive enactment, dependent on the will of a lawgiver and the extrinsic sanctions which he has attached to its observance. Let us take the claim in the form in which it is presented by Kant, by Butler, or by Sidgwick, each of whom acknowledges, and indeed emphasizes, the absolute character of duty, irrespective of

[1] At certain stages of civilization, when the population seems sharply divided between the oppressors and the oppressed, or between the selfish rich and the helpless poor, this feeling prompts men to figure the after-life as a simple reversal of the arrangements from which they had suffered here.

consequences to ourselves either in this life or another. The categorical imperative admits of no by-ends; virtue for Kant would cease to be virtue if it were not absolutely disinterested. 'Duty', Sidgwick wrote, 'is to me as real a thing as the physical world, though it is not apprehended in the same way.'[1] Nevertheless Kant goes on to say that the *summum bonum*, the whole and perfect good, the ultimate object of desire, is not virtue alone, but virtue and happiness together. These are two elements, 'specifically distinct' but 'necessarily united in one concept', in the sense that virtue must bring happiness in its train. Happiness is, of course, to be taken here not in the sense of the mental satisfaction and peace which is the normal consequence of virtuous action in the mind of the agent; according to Kant's definition a little later, 'happiness is the condition of a rational being in the world with whom everything goes according to his wish and will'. The synthesis of virtue and happiness so understood is obviously not realized in the present world. It is required, nevertheless, Kant maintains, 'not merely in the partial eyes of the person who makes himself an end, but even in the judgement of an impartial reason which regards persons in general as ends in themselves. For to need happiness, to deserve it, and yet at the same time not to participate in it, cannot be consistent with the perfect volition of a rational Being who is at the same time all-powerful.' In this way Kant reaches the third Postulate of the Practical Reason, the existence of God, as a being able to guarantee 'the exact harmony of happiness with morality' which constitutes the morally perfect world—or, as he puts it again, a Being able to guarantee 'the distribution of happiness in exact proportion to morality'.[2]

[1] *Memoir*, p. 347.

[2] The quotations are from the 'Dialectic of Pure Practical Reason', chap. ii, and will be found in Abbott's translation, *Kant's Theory of Ethics*, pp. 206–31.

Sidgwick, at the conclusion of his *Methods of Ethics*, is equally emphatic on the necessity of correlating virtue and happiness, and on the 'irrationality' of a world in which the harmony is not realized. Accepting as equally self-evident the axiom of egoistic hedonism, that it is ultimately reasonable to seek one's own happiness, and the axiom on which Utilitarianism had proceeded, without formulating it, 'that it is right and reasonable for me to treat others as I should think that I myself ought to be treated under similar conditions, and to do what I believe to be ultimately conducive to Universal Good or Happiness',[1] he finds himself obliged to acknowledge that, in our experience, the two principles may and do conflict. Hence, he concludes, 'the whole system of our beliefs as to the intrinsic reasonableness of conduct must fall, without a hypothesis, unverifiable by experience, reconciling the individual with the Universal Reason, without a belief, in some form or other, that the moral order which we see imperfectly realized in this actual world is yet actually perfect. If we reject this belief . . . the Cosmos of Duty is really reduced to a Chaos; and the prolonged effort of the human intellect to frame a perfect ideal of rational conduct is seen to have been foredoomed to inevitable failure.'[2]

The juxtaposition of Kant's and Sidgwick's statements seems to me to illuminate their common presuppositions. Both professedly confine themselves to morality as

[1] *Methods of Ethics*, p. 503 (3rd ed.).

[2] The exact words of this passage are quoted from the first edition of the *Methods* in 1874. The phraseology of the concluding paragraphs of the book was refashioned in subsequent editions, chiefly, I think, because Sidgwick wished to confine his treatise strictly to Ethics and to avoid the appearance of actually making Kant's theistic postulate. But he asserts quite as definitely in the later editions, that such a hypothesis is 'logically necessary to avoid a fundamental contradiction in one chief department of our thought'—a universe being 'fundamentally irrational' 'in which "Good for the individual" is not identified with "Universal Good"' (3rd. ed., p. 504. Cf. *Memoir*, pp. 347, 472, 605).

distinguished from religion, and both discuss the question (to quote a phrase of Sidgwick's) 'from the standpoint of the reflective individual'.[1] The question which the individual raises is—'Why should I, always and in all circumstances, do what is most conducive to the well-being of my society or of humanity at large?' And it is assumed that he cannot 'rationalize' his conduct unless he can show that it is in every case his 'interest' as an individual to act as 'social duty' requires. But in reality to put such a question is to fall from the moral standpoint altogether. It is simply the question 'Why should I be moral?', and as Mr. Bradley pointed out long ago in *Ethical Studies*, that question contains a hidden dogma. It rests on the assumption that virtue is a mere means to some ulterior end, happiness being here the end taken for granted. But this abolishes morality altogether, as understood by the moral consciousness; for 'that consciousness, when unwarped by selfishness and not blinded by sophistry, is convinced that to ask for the Why? is simple immorality; to do good for its own sake is virtue, to do it for some ulterior end or object, not itself good, is never virtue.'[2]

And again, the conflict between individual and social good could present itself as 'a fundamental contradiction' only to a theory which separated the individual in a wholly illegitimate way from the society whose traditions and customs have made him what he is, and with which, in all the main concerns of life, he feels himself indissolubly one. Whether we look at the matter historically or philosophically, morality is rooted in the idea of a *common* good. The moral person is not an exclusive individual, a bundle of sensitive desires and satisfactions; he is the organ of a common reason, and it is no mere metaphor to say that we are members one of another. This is a theme

[1] *Memoir*, p. 605.

[2] *Ethical Studies*, p. 56.

on which I need not enlarge, for ethical theory has moved rapidly during the last fifty years, and the individualism of Kant and Sidgwick seems already comparatively remote. The difficulties which that individualism made for itself receive no countenance from the workings of the moral consciousness in the plain man. Men face death for their country or for any great cause, they risk their lives to rescue an unknown stranger, they toil unceasingly to relieve the sick and the suffering, without a thought of personal reward. They are embarassed by praise or thanks; 'What else could I do?' they will reply, 'anybody else would have done the same.'

And if the idea of merit is foreign to the genuinely moral consciousness, the very idea of 'justice' as the satisfaction of an individual 'right' seems to disappear in the atmosphere of religion; 'service', 'sacrifice', 'brotherhood' are the terms which take its place. This is convincingly argued by Professor Bosanquet in a fine chapter on 'The World of Claims and Counter Claims',[1] to which I would refer you. In religion, he argues, we have left that world—the world of 'abstract justice' or 'individual apportionment'—the justice of the law courts—far behind us. The member of a spiritual whole is one with the 'child, the beggar, the criminal, the revolutionist. They may throw horrible burdens on him and he has to shoulder them.' And such burdens 'will continually be borne in chief measure by "the best"—"the completest, most capable, least obviously guilty members of the whole".' This, as he reminds us, is the 'fundamental truth of the doctrine of vicarious atonement'. It is a principle exemplified instinctively in our arrangements for any difficult and important enterprise. 'We do not give the "best man" the most comfortable, the easiest task . . . we give him the greatest responsibility, the severest toil and hazard,

[1] *Value and Destiny of the Individual*, Lect. V.

the most continuous and exacting work and self-sacrifice.' At such a level, the call so to do and to suffer is not felt as a hardship; it is valued as a privilege. Hence the whole idea of the future life as required to redress the balance of this life, as a compensation to individuals for their undeserved sufferings or, in Dr. McDougall's words, for 'the bitter injustices'[1] to which they have been subjected, seems without basis in moral and religious experience. It is wonderful, indeed, to see how extreme pain or bodily infirmity, so inexplicable in their incidence on any principles of moral desert, are 'accepted', as we say, by simple people who make no special profession of religion—accepted as part of the ordinance of nature, without a thought of personal wrong done them or any idea of posthumous compensation. If such ideas are not present to the mind of the sufferers themselves, it may well be that 'the reflective moralist', when, in the role of impartial spectator, he lodges a claim on their behalf, has mistaken the true inwardness of the situation.

If this line of thought is true, it will follow that neither the idea of retribution nor that of compensation is a sufficient foundation on which to build a theory of a future life. Punishment for punishment's sake is barren, and the claim for compensation or reward, in the ordinary sense of these terms, does not seem to form part of the moral or religious consciousness itself. I have already argued, in discussing the doctrine of Karma, that we impoverish the universe if we regard it primarily as a mechanism for grinding out rewards and punishments. We may be profoundly convinced, with Carlyle, that 'the great soul of the world is just'; but distributive justice, conceived in the fashion we have been considering, is altogether too finite and legal a thing—one might almost

[1] *Body and Mind*, p. 356.

say too petty a thing—to be the central fact or business of the universe.

I cannot admit, therefore, that, if the hope of immortality were withdrawn, the moral foundations of the world would crumble to pieces. While I certainly think that the denial of human survival must profoundly affect our general view of the world, I cannot agree that the doctrine of immortality is, as some would make it, the absolutely central article of a philosophic or religious creed. There are those who say roundly that without a future life there can be no morality. 'If you believe in no future life', says Luther, in a peculiarly coarse and violent outburst, 'I would not give a mushroom for your God. Do then as you like. For, if no God, then no devil, no hell. As with a fallen tree, all is over when you die. Then plunge into lechery, rascality, robbery and murder.'[1] Less violently, but to the same effect, Massillon, the French preacher: 'If we wholly perish with the body, the maxims of charity, patience, justice, honour, gratitude and friendship are but empty words. Our passions shall decide our duty. If retribution terminate with the grave, morality is a mere chimera, a bugbear of human invention.'[2] Even St. Paul's famous resurrection argument is infected by the same idea. 'If in this life only we have hope in Christ, we are of all men most miserable. . . . What advantageth it me, if the dead rise not? Let us eat and drink, for to-morrow we die.' But though he may argue thus, St. Paul, we need not doubt, would have drawn for himself W. K. Clifford's nobler conclusion: 'Do I seem to say, "Let us eat and drink, for to-morrow we die?" Far from it; on the contrary I say: Let us take hands and help, for this day we are alive together.'[3]

[1] Quoted by Alger, p. 654.
[2] *Œuvres complètes*, tome 13.
[3] *Lectures and Essays*, i, p. 226.

Of those who reason like Luther, 'If no God, then no devil, no hell', as if the latter were the really important point—of them and of their logic we need speak no further. We have heard the words of Plato and Spinoza on the subject in a previous lecture, and Milton's lines may here suffice:

> Virtue could see to do what Virtue would
> By her own radiant light, though sun and moon
> Were in the flat sea sunk.[1]

But there are many who would not put such conclusions in practice, who do not in fact regard the reasoning as logically valid, but who yet fear that, if the sanctions of a future life were removed, the mass of mankind would, as a matter of fact, reason in that way and plunge into universal licence. Dr. McDougall, for instance, thinks it 'highly probable that the passing away of this belief would be calamitous for our civilization'. He 'gravely doubts' whether without it 'whole nations could rise to the level of an austere morality, or even maintain a decent standard of conduct'.[2] Renan is still more emphatic: 'The day in which the belief in an after-life shall vanish from the earth will witness a terrific moral and spiritual decadence. Some of us, perhaps, could do without it, provided only that others held it fast. But there is no lever capable of raising an entire people, if once they have lost their faith in the immortality of the soul.'[3] But this is surely to forget that the national life of the Jewish people, although not of course destitute of all religious sanction, was notoriously for long without any theory of the future life as bearing upon conduct in the present; and the same held true, as we saw, of the

[1] *Comus*, 373-5.

[2] *Body and Mind*, Preface.

[3] Quoted by Archdeacon Charles in his Drew Lecture on *Immortality*, p. 4.

shadowy animistic beliefs of the Greeks and Romans during centuries of their most vigorous life.

> Nos ubi decidimus
> quo pater Aeneas, quo dives Tullus et Ancus,
> pulvis et umbra sumus.[1]

The civilization of these nations may have been inferior at important points to our own, but that 'a decent standard' of family and social life was maintained, there can be no reasonable doubt. The old Roman virtue passed into a proverb. So far as restraint upon the baser elements of a population is concerned, we must also remember that this must always depend upon the crude and immediate sanctions of the criminal law and the pressure of public opinion. Hence we may be reasonably confident, with Sidgwick, that 'morality can take care of itself, or rather [he adds] the principle of life in human society can take care of morality'.[2] But we shall be agreed, I fancy, that to argue for the indispensability of the doctrine, merely as a check upon our own passions or as a kind of police protection against the worse excesses of others, is hardly an adequate way of handling a professedly religious belief.

Let us look at the question, then, more broadly; and, to simplify the argument, let us confine it to the case of a blessed immortality. Have we any right to stake the whole character of the universe as rational and righteous on the question of our personal survival or non-survival? The attitude, when so stated, seems incongruous and even unseemly; yet Professor Taylor concludes, in an essay on 'The Belief in Immortality', written during the War, that 'pessimistic atheism' seems to him 'the only logical alternative to the Christian faith'.[3] But

[1] Horace, *Odes*, iv. 7. Cf. i. 4. [2] *Memoir*, p. 472.

[3] Cf. the volume of essays published under the title, *The Faith and the War*, p. 149.

there is no warrant for setting up, as Professor Taylor there does, an ostensibly exhaustive alternative between a universe that guarantees immortality and a 'stupid and immoral' universe, that is to say, the universe of materialism. That truth, goodness, and beauty are revealed as values in the world as we know it, is a simple fact of experience; and to have seen and known these eternal values makes it forever impossible to think of the world of birth and death in any other light than as the vehicle of their manifestation. Professor Taylor's position is the same as Tennyson's in the violent outburst to which I referred in my Aberdeen lectures on the *Idea of God*.[1] 'If immortality be not true,' he said, and as he spoke he grew crimson with excitement, 'then no God but a mocking fiend created us.... I'd sink my head to-night in a chloroformed handkerchief and have done with it all.' No attitude, surely, could be more irreligious. I quoted then, by way of contrast, a fine passage from Dr. Hutchison Stirling, the distinguished philosopher who was the first Gifford Lecturer appointed in Scotland. Let me recall now the noble and truly religious words of Epictetus in contemplation of death:

'What then would you have death find you doing? For my part I would be found busy with some humane task, whatever it be—something noble, beneficent, advancing the common weal. And if I cannot be found doing great things like these, I would do what none can hinder, what is given me to do, setting myself right, working to achieve freedom from passion, rendering what is due in every relation of life. ... If death finds me thus occupied, I am content if I can lift up my hands to God and say, 'I have not neglected the faculties which I received from Thee, to enable me to understand Thy governance and follow it, I have not dishonoured Thee as far as in me lay. ... Have I ever murmured at aught that came to pass, or wished it otherwise? In that Thou didst beget me, I am grateful for thy gifts; in so far as I have used what thou gavest me, I am satisfied. Take thy gifts back

[1] p. 44.

again and place them where thou wilt; for they were all Thine, Thou gavest them me'.[1]

Epictetus had been a slave and he was lame; so that we must not imagine that a spoiled favourite of fortune is speaking. He is thinking of the great simple things that make it good to have lived. 'Beholding the sun, moon and stars, enjoying earth and sea', he says in another passage, 'a man is neither helpless nor alone.'[2]

The Stoic philosophy is the standing refutation of Professor Taylor's alternative; for it combined profound faith in a divine Reason, ordering all things aright, with a complete absence of belief in personal immortality. I have already referred to the other historical instance of the Hebrews. 'The Old Testament', says Sir George Adam Smith, 'is of use in reminding us that the hope of immortality is one of the secondary and inferential elements of religious experience.'[3] I said, therefore, ten years ago, and I still think, 'that we place an exaggerated emphasis upon human immortality, if we make it the centre and foundation of our whole world-theory'. We should observe a due proportion and order in our reasoning. The order of our going must be from God to man and not vice versa. Our conclusions as to the value and destiny of the

[1] *Discourses*, Bk. IV, c. 10.

[2] Cf. R. L. Stevenson, 'The House Beautiful':

> To make this earth, our hermitage,
> A cheerful and a changeful page,
> God's bright and intricate device
> Of days and seasons doth suffice.

[3] *Modern Criticism and the Preaching of the Old Testament*, p. 176. Principal Galloway expresses the same view temperately and well: 'If by postulate we mean something upon which the existence of the religious life depends, then immortality is not a postulate in this sense. For a religion may exist and has existed where there was no belief in a future life. On the other hand, if we take the term postulate in a wider way to denote a hypothesis which gives deeper meaning and value both to religious and ethical experience, and which helps to reconcile contradictions, then the doctrine of immortality deserves the name of a postulate' (*Principles of Religious Development*, p. 342).

individual must ultimately depend upon our conception of God and his relation to his creatures. If we can reach any positive convictions, they will be based, not upon man's claims, real or supposed, but upon the perfection of God and his nature as Love.

And just here, I think, we touch the difference between the Stoic and what we may call the Christian mood. Stoicism, it has been said, was 'the offspring of despair'.[1] The break-up of the old Greek city-states under the Macedonian Empire left no scope for free political activity; and the individual, finding no external sphere in which he could realize his life, was forced to retreat within himself and seek an internal satisfaction in the discipline of his will and the ensuing sense of superiority to the worst that circumstances can inflict upon him. The whole sphere of the external is thus surrendered, and he retreats upon his 'unconquerable soul'—

> I am the master of my fate:
> I am the captain of my soul.

There is even an element of defiance in his mood, like that reflected in Henley's lines. But it does not become dominant; for, if suffering is not really an evil, we cannot permanently cherish indignation against its infliction. The authentic Stoic ideal is, therefore, Apatheia, the passionless calm in which the wise man rises superior to the sundry and manifold changes of the world. But, just as the original individualism of the Stoics—the abstention from civic and national life forced upon them by the political circumstances of the time—became transformed into the positive idea of the brotherhood of all men and a citizenship of the universe, so the earlier attitude of self-sufficient superiority passed into one of religious acquiescence based on a theory of the divine government

[1] Lightfoot's paper on 'St. Paul and Seneca', appended to his commentary on the Epistle to the Philippians.

of the world. The passage from the one attitude to the other is intelligible, because the idea of a universal reason or divine law was an essential constituent of the Stoic creed. Epictetus and Marcus Aurelius may be said to be only giving a personal application to what was so nobly hymned in general terms by Cleanthes. Still the difference of temper between the founders of the school and the later generation is marked. The later representatives of the school insist as strongly as their predecessors on the inner freedom which makes a man independent of circumstances; but with Epictetus and Marcus Aurelius this inward freedom and peace is not the result of a barren withdrawal into the citadel of self. It seems always to be reached through the thought of 'that great community which consists of God and man'[1]—the 'city of God' of which both Epictetus and Marcus so often speak—so that the pains and the misfortunes of the individual appear at times almost as a vicarious suffering of the parts for the whole. They are to be accepted, at all events, uncomplainingly, even joyously, as factors which are integral to the harmony of the whole. 'I am in harmony with all that is,' says Marcus, 'a part of thy harmony, great Universe. For me nothing is too early and nothing too late that is in season for thee.'[2] 'My will', says Epictetus, 'is simply that which comes to pass, for I consider what God wills better than what I will.'[3] And just in proportion as the relation between the individual and this all-ruling Providence became more personal, in proportion as the idea of impersonal Law, Necessity or Fate, gives place to that of Fatherhood, the question tends to arise, as we saw it did among the Jews, whether it is compatible with the idea of fatherly love and care that the relation of conscious

[1] Epictetus, *Discourses*, Bk. I, c. 9.
[2] *Meditations*, Bk. VI. iv. 23.
[3] *Discourses*, Bk. IV, c. 7.

sonship, to which Epictetus and Seneca so often appeal, should be abruptly terminated by death.

'In proportion to spiritual progress', says Dr. Dill, 'is the force of spiritual longings.'[1] There is a poignant passage, towards the close of his *Meditations*, in which Marcus Aurelius puts the question, 'How can it be that the gods who ordered all things well and lovingly, overlooked this one thing, that some men, and very good men—men, who, as we may say, have had most communion with the divinity, and through pious acts and observances have been most intimate with the divinity—when they have once died, should never renew their being, but should be utterly extinguished.'[2] Marcus found no answer, yet he does not permit the apparent anomaly to shake his firmly based faith in the divine Reason and Providence that rules the world. I know few passages nobler in attitude than the simple sentences which follow, in which we seem to hear him reasoning with his own doubt. 'But if this be truly so, be assured that, if it ought to have been otherwise, the gods would have made it otherwise. Had it been right, it would have been practicable, and if it had been according to nature, nature would have had it so. But since it is not so (if in fact it is not so), be persuaded that it ought not to have been. For thou seest even of thyself that, in debating this matter, thou art pleading a point of justice with the gods, and we should not thus plead with the gods, were they not perfectly good and just. And if that is so, they would not have allowed anything to be unjustly or unreasonably neglected, in the ordering of the universe.' But although he thus retreats upon the high doctrine of his school, the mere fact of the question is significant of the failure of his creed to satisfy his own highest conception of the divine character and procedure.

[1] *Roman Society from Nero to Marcus Aurelius*, p. 391.
[2] *Meditations*, Bk. XII. 5.

I venture to think that something of the same kind may be detected in the writings of our modern Stoics, who, while preaching like their predecessors the perfection of the whole, insist, as we saw in a previous lecture, on the essentially transient function of the finite individuals in whom 'the Absolute lives a little and for a little time'. 'The atmosphere of our pilgrimage', says Professor Bosanquet, in the concluding sentences of his second volume of Gifford lectures, 'has necessarily been sombre.'[1] 'The universe', he says, in the same chapter, 'is a rough place', that is, for its finite inhabitants; and a large part of the volume had been devoted to what he calls 'the hazards and hardships of finite self-hood'. There is undoubtedly much that is salutary in his insistence on the necessary severity of the soul-forming process. The pervading atmosphere is due, in part at least, to the sincerity of the treatment, to a praiseworthy desire to face the facts of the universe and to accept no merely sentimental solution of the difficulties. But it is impossible to doubt that the main reason of the sombreness which he confesses is an underlying sense—at least in his readers—of the inhumanity of a universe which moulds souls so painfully, only to break them up again. And to say inhuman is to say undivine; for we have no other standard of the divine than the best that we can think or feel. All honour to those who prefer to subsist on starvation rations rather than feed on 'boundless hopes'[2] which they deem too good to be true. But it does not follow that their judgement is correct: the truth may be something larger and better than their theory has room for.

[1] *Value and Destiny*, p. 327.

[2] Matthew Arnold's Sonnet, 'The Better Part'.

LECTURE X

CONCLUSIONS

THE defect of the Stoic theory, whether in its ancient or its modern form, is ultimately to be found, as I argued in the preceding lecture, in the subordination of persons to impersonal values. But Truth, Beauty, Goodness have no reality as self-existent abstractions; they have no meaning apart from conscious experience. They carry us therefore to a primal Mind in whose experience they are eternally realized. God himself is at once the supreme Reality and, as Dante calls him, the supreme Value—*il primo, il summo Valore.*[1] And the highest conception we can form of perfect personality is Love, not in any shallow sentimental sense, but the self-giving Love which expends itself for others, and lives in all their joys and sorrows. Such love, then, the principle of our argument bids us take as the ultimate value of which the universe is the manifestation. It bids us conceive the inmost being of God not solely as the realization of eternal Truth and the enjoyment of perfect Beauty, but pre-eminently as the exercise and fruition of his nature as Love. And if so, the value of the finite world to the Spirit of the universe must lie, above all else, if one may so speak with modesty and reverence, in the spirits to whom he has given the capacity to make themselves in his own image. The spirits themselves must be the values to God, not simply the degrees of intelligence and virtue, abstractly considered, which they respectively realize. They are not

[1] So Nicholas of Cusa describes God as *valor valorum*. Cf. Dean Inge's *Philosophy of Plotinus*, ii. 127.

made, then—we seem justified in concluding—to be broken up and cast aside and to be replaced by relays of others in a continual succession.

Here again, as throughout, we are applying the idea of the divine perfection, appealing for the interpretation of the more and the less perfect to our own experience. I remember many years ago reading a little book by one of our minor poets, in which he expounded with some complacency what he called 'The Religion of a Literary Man'. Among other serious topics which he handled was that of the Hereafter, in its bearing on friendship and the death of friends. 'We love our friends', he argued, 'not, as we often say, "for themselves", but for their possession of certain qualities, for their good nature, their wit, their beauty, or whatever their qualities may be; and these qualities are to be met with over and over again, possibly in still more satisfying harmonies. Thus we have not to wait to meet our old friends again in heaven, we meet them again already on earth—in the new ones.' The rest of the book I have quite forgotten, but this sentiment has remained in my memory as a signal instance of poverty of feeling and shallowness of nature. The application of the reminiscence is obvious. Are we to attribute to the divine Friend and Lover of men a levity of attitude which we find offensively untrue of our ordinary human fidelities? Are we to liken Him to a military commander, who is content if fresh drafts are forthcoming to fill his depleted battalions? To the military system, men are only so much human material, so many numerable units; but a chance encounter with one of the men in the flesh, one touch of human-heartedness, is sufficient to dissolve the abstraction which so regards them.

Many voices bid us distrust a hope which, they tell us, is but the phantom offspring of our own desire. What is it, they say, but the old dream of a golden age, whether figured in the past or returning still more glorious in the future?

> Fools! that so often here
> Happiness mock'd our prayer,
> I think, might make us fear
> A like event elsewhere!
> Make us, not fly to dreams, but moderate desire.[1]

There is ground for the warning. But everything depends on the nature of the desire. Those who think of heaven primarily as a place where all hardship shall cease, where no exertion shall be needed, but every harmless longing frustrated in the present life shall receive its fullest gratification, may well be preparing for themselves a disappointment. There are no signs that the universe is conducted on hedonistic principles, and just for that reason it appears to the hedonist 'a sorry scheme'.[2] Desire in itself is irresponsible; seeing only its own object, it is blind to all the larger ends which are incompatible with its demands. So long, therefore, as it remains the desire of private satisfaction, no such desire can be regarded as secure of fulfilment. The existence of the very general, if not universal, desire of immortality is sometimes adduced as itself a powerful argument for the belief that the desire will be satisfied. But so long as it remains simply a desire for personal continuance—an instinctive shrinking from death—we cannot build upon it in the way suggested. Desire, at such a level, has no lien upon the universe; unless it be purged of its original selfishness, it can be no guide to us in such a question. The familiar message of religion everywhere is renunciation, death to self, as the gateway to freedom and to the wider life which is life indeed. The desires of the religious man are, therefore, for 'the brethren' rather than for himself—for himself only as one with them, a member of what Royce

[1] Matthew Arnold, *Empedocles on Etna.*

[2] Omar Khayyám.

called[1] 'the blessed community'; and in a large sense the object of their corporate desire may be said to be an increasing knowledge of God and of his will. At such a standpoint, the belief in immortality is not based by the religious man on any personal claim for himself or even for others; it seems rather, as our argument has suggested, to be an inference from the character of God.

In an old novel of George Macdonald's there is quoted an epitaph in doggerel verse—

> Here lie I, Martin Elginbrod:
> Hae mercy o' my soul, Lord God;
> As I wad dae, were I Lord God,
> And ye were Martin Elginbrod.

The sentiment of the lines is unimpeachable, but the standard of conduct is pitched too low. The principle is stated with a diviner breadth in the 'how much more' of the Gospels. 'If ye then, being evil, know how to give good gifts unto your children, how much more shall your Father which is in Heaven give good things to them that ask him.'[2] 'Too good to be true' is a saying often on our lips; and the mood it expresses is on the whole a prudent one, when it is a case of worldly goods and prospects. But, as some one has said,[3] 'too good *not* to be true' is the more fitting expression, where it is a question of the ultimate ideals and hopes which have been the nursing-fathers and nursing-mothers of mankind. For serious philosophical reflection nothing can be more foolish than the common talk which tries to set these down as the baseless dreams of subjective fancy—as if man were self-created, and as if he developed his ideals in the internal vacancy of his individual mind. Man can no more rise spiritually above himself in his own strength than he can raise himself from

[1] In *The Problem of Christianity*.

[2] Matt. vii. 11.

[3] Sir Henry Jones, in his volume on Browning, quotes the saying as Emerson's, but I have been unable to verify the reference.

the ground by tugging at his own shoulder-straps. We did not make ourselves, and we do not weave our ideals out of nothing. They are all derived; they point to their source in a real Perfection, in which is united all that, and more than, it hath entered into the heart of man to conceive. The essential meaning of the old ontological argument, I have argued elsewhere,[1] is that the best we think, or can think, must *be*.

'A strange mystery it is', says Mr. Bertrand Russell,[2] 'that Nature, omnipotent but blind, in the revolutions of her secular hurryings through the abysses of space, has brought forth at last a child, subject still to her power, but gifted with sight, with knowledge of good and evil, with the capacity of judging all the works of his unthinking Mother.' And he proceeds to explain how God is the 'creation of our own conscience', 'created by our own love of the good', and to tell us that it is for man to 'worship at the shrine that his own hands have built', although well aware that the Deity within has no being in the actual world. A strange mystery indeed! The mystery rather is that Mr. Russell should apparently never have brought his philosophical reflection to bear upon the sheer incredibility of the supposition—the idea of a complete absence of relation between the world of fact and the world of values, the world of fact or reality consisting solely of 'the blind empire of matter', and the world of values being a world of phantoms produced by autosuggestion in the brain of one of the casual products of this 'omnipotent matter' as it 'rolls on in its relentless way'. If we refuse to entertain so extravagant a hypothesis, we shall not be reduced to building our soul's habitation, as Mr. Russell advises us, 'on the firm foundation of unyielding despair'. We shall believe that here,

[1] *Idea of God*, p. 241.

[2] In his essay, 'The Free Man's Worship' (*Philosophical Essays*, p. 61 *et seq.*).

as elsewhere, nothing comes from nothing—that whatever elements of goodness exist in us must have their source in the Power that brought us into being, and that the ideals of unattained perfection to which we reach forward are due to the same inspiration. On this, which seems the only reasonable view, the permanent ideals which have lighted mankind on its way must be taken as our best clue to the inmost nature of the real, and even the so-called instinct of immortality will not lose its legitimate significance. For we may say without exaggeration that it is man's meditation upon death that has made him, and makes him, the human creature he is. His philosophy, his religion, his greatest poetry, all have their roots in the fact of death and in his refusal to accept it as final. The central and beneficent function of death in human experience has been finely expressed by Hawthorne: 'What a blessing to mortals,' he wrote,[1] 'what a kindness of Providence, that life is made so uncertain, that Death is thrown in among the possibilities of our being. For without it, how would it be possible to be heroic, how we should plod along in commonplace for ever! . . . God gave the whole world to man, and if he is left alone with it, it will make a clod of him at last; but to remedy that, God gave man a grave, and it redeems all, and makes an immortal spirit of him in the end.'

It does not follow, however, that we are to think of personal immortality as an inherent possession of every human soul, or a talismanic gift conferred indiscriminately on every being born in human shape. We talk very loosely of 'souls' and 'persons', as if these were static entities, magically called into being, and complete from the outset. But it is manifestly a question of degree: *how much* personality, how much of a coherent soul has the

[1] In an unfinished novel. The passage is quoted in Edward Caird's *Lay Sermons*, p. 272.

experience of life developed within the animal creature? For personality or selfhood is not anything that can be conferred by another, it is emphatically something that must be won before there can be any question of its conservation. What is given is simply the opportunity. A true self comes into being as the result of continuous effort, and the same effort is needed to hold it together and ensure its maintenance; for the danger of disintegration is always present.

> Nur der verdient die Freiheit wie das Leben
> Der täglich sie erobern muss.[1]

If a man is no more than a loosely associated group of appetites and habits, the self as a moral unity has either flickered out or has never yet come into existence. To the constitution of such a real self there must go some persistent purpose, or rather some coherent system of aims and ideals, and some glimpse at least, it would seem, of the eternal values. Eternal life, as a present experience, lent no support, we saw, to the view that such experience is limited to the present life, nor to the view that it tends in any way to bring about its own cessation by dissolving the finite personality. It does, however, certainly suggest that the further life is to be regarded as the sequel and the harvest of what began here. Plato speaks, in the *Republic*[2], of souls that pass through life in a kind of stupor: 'Dreaming and drowsing this present life through, before ever awaking here, they are gone to Hades to the final sleep.' How should such earth-bound souls

> Support the fervours of the heavenly morn?
> No, no! The energy of life may be
> Kept on after the grave, but not begun;
> And he who flagged not in the earthly strife,
> From strength to strength advancing—only he,
> His soul well-knit, and all his battles won,
> Mounts, and that hardly, to eternal life.[3]

[1] Goethe, *Faust*, Part II. Faust's words immediately before his death.
[2] Bk. VII. 534.
[3] Matthew Arnold's Sonnet, 'Immortality'.

Dante is confronted by the problem of the characterless soul at the outset of his journey—the multitude of those who in their life-time 'were never alive', who lived 'without praise or blame', 'taking part neither for God nor for his enemies'. Chased forth from Heaven and rejected by Hell, these spirits hover in Dante's imagination on the hither side of Acheron. 'The world suffers no rumour of them to survive; mercy disdains them, and justice too. Let us not talk of them, but look and pass.' Dante was obliged to find a place for them because of the Catholic dogma of the natural immortality of every soul. But why should the universe be permanently burdened by the continued existence of those who made no use of life while they had it? People talk as if the being of a soul were something which almost defied annihilation, which at any rate could be brought to an end only by a special fiat of the Deity. But surely it is quite the other way. It is but a relaxing of central control, and a process of dissociation at once begins. Nothing seems more fatally easy than the dissolution in this fashion of the coherent unity which we call a mind, if the process is allowed to continue and to spread. We can observe the phenomenon frequently in cases of disease, when it affects the practical activities of life; but the mere relaxation of moral effort may initiate the same process in the spiritual sphere. And without the unity implied in some continuous purpose, what prospect can there be of eternal life, or what meaning can it have?

It is not as if intellectual distinction, or distinguished achievement of any kind, were demanded as a passport to the heavenly kingdom. In one of his symbolic utterances in the second part of *Faust*, Goethe says

> Wer keinen Namen sich erwarb, noch Edles will,
> Gehört den Elementen an.[1]

[1] The words are those of the leader of the chorus in *Helena*, dismissing the spirits.

'He who won himself no name and wills no noble end, returns to the elements as their lawful prey.' But, as if conscious that the criterion, so expressed, savours too much of the aristocracy of genius, he adds at once:

> Nicht nur Verdienst, auch Treue wahrt uns die Person.

'Not only merit or desert, fidelity also—the faithful heart—preserves for us our personality.' Some little unremembered act of kindness ('Lord, when saw we thee an hungred, and fed thee? or thirsty, and gave thee drink?'), some dim perception of the sacred beauty of unselfish affection, the uncomplaining acceptance of hardship with no envy of those more fortunately placed, some sense, perhaps, of nature's environing beauty and peace—

> the unassuming things that hold
> A silent station in this beauteous world—

of such simplicities is the Kingdom of Heaven. What further credentials are needed for the eternal citizenship? And who will presume to declare them absent even in

> Souls that appear to have no depth at all
> To careless eyes?

Intelligence, on the contrary, merely as such, if employed simply for finite and selfish ends, though it be what we call human as distinguished from animal intelligence, carries with it no promise of a further life. Man, if we look at him as entirely absorbed in his finite activities, is no fit subject for immortality; there is no more call to raise the question in his case than in the case of other animals. This is the key to Hume's negative treatment of the subject in his unpublished essay on the Immortality of the Soul. Professor Ward has remarked that Hume's suppression of this essay is not to be wondered at, seeing that 'its arguments rest on a cynical and ignoble estimate of humanity that has seldom been surpassed'.[1] The reason

[1] *Realm of Ends*, p. 386*n*.

is, as I have suggested, that Hume del
his survey to man's biological activities as a m
animal species. Looking at him thus, he concludes
'if any purpose of nature be clear, we may affirm that the whole scope and intention of man's creation, so far as we can judge by natural reason, is limited to the present life... If the reason of man gives him a great superiority over other animals, his necessities are proportionally multiplied upon him. His whole time, his whole capacity, activity, courage, passion, find sufficient employment in fencing against the miseries of his present condition, and frequently, nay almost always, are too slender for the business assigned them... The powers of men are no more superior to their wants, considered merely in this life, than those of foxes and hares are, compared to *their* wants and to *their* period of existence. The inference from parity of reasoning is therefore obvious.'

Certainly, if reason were no more than this—a more effective weapon in the struggle for existence—Hume's argument would hold: man's life would be altogether on the same scale as that of foxes and hares, his outlook and activities limited, like theirs, to the present scene. There is nothing here to differentiate reason from instinct; one or two instincts thrown in might have served the purpose more effectively. But Hume deliberately ignores the fact that it is just by the operation of reason that the finite completeness of the merely animal life is broken up. 'A spark disturbs our clod' and 'projects the soul on its lone way',

> A man, for aye removed
> From the developed brute; a god though in the germ.[1]

To identify reason with the computative understanding, and to limit the field of its operation to the economic struggle, is gratuitously and unwarrantably to impoverish the meaning of the word. Art and science, morality and

[1] Browning, 'Rabbi ben Ezra'.

n, all have their roots in reason, and these are to us charter of our common humanity. The perception beauty—the whole range of aesthetic emotion and artistic practice, from the cave man onwards—is quite useless for the preservation of the individual or of the species. Scientific truth may certainly be applied as serviceable knowledge; but the pursuit of truth for truth's sake, which is the inspiration of science, is unaffected by such material inducements. Bacon's philosophy predisposed him to emphasize the practical function of knowledge, the inventions to which it gives rise for the development of the 'regnum hominis' and 'the relief of man's estate'; yet he tells us that 'without doubt the contemplation of things as they are, without superstition or imposture, without error or confusion, is in itself a nobler thing than the whole harvest of inventions'.[1] 'God hath framed the mind of man as a mirror or glass, capable of the image of the universal world, and joyful to receive the impression thereof, as the eye joyeth to receive light.'[2] Truth, Beauty, and Goodness: in view of man's admission to worlds like these it becomes the merest travesty of the facts—I would say a mere affectation—to ignore, as naturalism does, the difference in scale between such a life and that of any of his animal compeers. For the difference is not quantitative—not merely one of degree, that is to say—but qualitative and decisive. And it is just the discrepancy between human capacities and ideals and the limited opportunities of man's earthly existence that has throughout the history of the race so insistently suggested that the life we see must be only part of a larger plan.

And although immortality, as our argument has led us to think, is not something that comes to us automatically, but essentially something to be won and held, it would ill

[1] *Novum Organum*, Bk. I, Aphorism 129.

[2] *Advancement of Learning*, Bk. I. i. 3.

become us, in the phrase and the spirit of a bygone theology, to seek to limit the number of the elect, by making the destiny of any soul dependent on our finite and necessarily imperfect judgement of its character and possibilities. Better to bear in mind the words of Locke, when challenged by theological critics regarding the fate of 'changelings' in the other world: 'They are in the hands of a faithful Creator and a bountiful Father, who disposes not of his creatures according to our narrow thoughts and opinions, nor distinguishes them according to names and species of our contrivance. And we that know so little of this present world we are in, may I think content ourselves without being peremptory in defining the different states which creatures shall come into when they go off this stage.'[1] Our most peremptory judgements may often be the most fallacious. Are we not sometimes irritated by the unreasoning devotion of a woman—a wife or a mother—to a brute (as we say) whom every one else has given up as hopeless and would think the world well rid of? And yet that dumb fidelity and ever-repeated forgiveness of injuries depends on a faith in some spark of goodness in the wretch who appears to others so wholly vile. The faith and the love shame our impatience by the glimpse they seem to give us of the infinite long-suffering of a divine Compassion. It is rash to imagine that Patience exhausted in the short space of our earthly life. We know not what succession of experiences may be needed, before the vision of love and goodness awakens a degraded soul to the hideousness of its own condition. And it may be that, in the end, no single soul shall be 'cast as rubbish to the void, when God has made the pile complete'. There is hardly a more ignoble figure in literature than Peer Gynt, in the fifth Act of the play, hurrying from crossroad to

[1] *Essay*, Bk. IV. 4. 14. Changelings, in Locke's sense of the term, were creatures supposed to be half-man, half-beast.

crossroad to escape from the Button-moulder, who threatens to melt him up as old metal, because he has never been *himself* at all—his whole life having been a make-believe and a piece of selfish indulgence. The way in which he haggles to save his pitiful individuality only whets the reader's desire to see the just doom accomplished. And yet the poet saves him at the end. In a flash, in the light of Solveig's love, he sees things at last as they really are, and himself as he really is.[1]

The idea of a final restoration—the belief 'that somehow good will be the final goal of ill'—seems to many minds the belief most consonant with our idea of the divine perfection and the ultimately constraining power of the good. To think otherwise is, for Browning, to confess a failure of the divine plan for the soul in question; 'which must not be'.[2] It is the solution which commends itself to us as

[1] Cf. Browning's treatment of Guido in *The Ring and the Book*.

[2] The words of the aged Pope contemplating Guido's fate:

> So may the truth be flashed out by one blow,
> And Guido see, one instant, and be saved.
> Else I avert my face, nor follow him
> Into that sad, obscure, sequestered state
> Where God unmakes, but to remake, the soul
> He else made first in vain; which must not be.

The same view is emphatically supported by Sir Henry Jones in the volume of Gifford Lectures, *A Faith that Enquires*, published since his death. He thus summarizes his argument at the close of the lecture on Immortality: 'God is. God is perfect. His loving-kindness and power are unlimited; and his greatest gift to man is the gift of the power, tendency, and opportunity to learn goodness. God's goodness being unlimited, the opportunity not made use of by man in the present life is renewed for him in another life, and in still another; till, at last, his spirit finds rest in the service of the God of Love.' Any other hypothesis, he maintains, is inconsistent with the belief that 'the world-process is the expression of the sovereign will of a perfect Being' (p. 347). 'One genuine failure of the good in any one single life' would mean a failure of the divine purpose, and that would mean the entry of contingency and 'sheer unreason' into the universe, undermining even the postulate of order on which our ordinary scientific knowledge rests. 'This religious view of the world-process is that in the light of which alone the universe is left a cosmos and not a chaos' (p. 41). 'Denial of the immortality of the soul implies absolute Scepticism' (p. 347).

appropriate wherever a real self has come into being, were it only through rebellion and active sin. Spiritual energy may be shown in the pursuit of evil as well as of good. But what of the 'frustrate ghosts'[1] who have taken no sides, who seem never to have achieved selfhood by an act of personal choice at all? If we insist that every such 'soul' must go on for ever, are we not allowing ourselves to be swayed by the conception of a soul-thing created once for all by God? But there is no soul (in any sense relevant to our present question) except the unified personality built up by our own acts. In the absence of such a personality how can the question of an immortal destiny be properly said to arise? 'Ask, and it shall be given you; seek, and ye shall find.' It is contrary to every principle of the spiritual life to conceive of immortality as a gift thrust upon a man without his active co-operation. Those who have not known 'immortal longings' are not wronged if that is not granted which they have never sought.

The ideal of universal restoration, if it is allowed to harden into a dogma, involves a danger and may easily lay itself open to the same criticism as the vaunted law of automatic Progress in which the nineteenth century so profoundly believed. The operation of this natural law was to carry the race to ever higher heights, quite irrespective of the conscious co-operation of individuals, of their sluggish inertia or their open resistance. To proclaim universal restoration in similar fashion as a necessary law of the universe is to ignore the fact that, in the nature of the case, the destiny of a self-conscious spirit is committed to itself and depends upon a personal choice. To assure people that, whatever they do, all will come right in the end is not an effective method of awakening them to the gravity of decisions here and now, which bind

[1] Browning's own phrase in 'The Statue and the Bust'.

upon the soul the fetters of habit and make it ever more difficult to find the way back. But in fairness it must be admitted that, where the belief in ultimate restoration produces in the careless and impenitent the soporific effect apprehended, this result is really due to the idea of salvation not as a deliverance from sin, but as an escape from certain extrinsic penalties of sinning. When the appeal of the evangelist is made in the name of goodness itself, the idea of postponement to the future and of ultimately 'jinking' the consequences,[1] is one which will no longer arise.

In view of human freedom, it has sometimes been impressively contended that, although the good is freely offered to every soul, yet the possibility must always remain that some souls, however long their probation, may, to the end, harden their hearts against the divine appeal, and so by their own act exclude themselves from grace. But on full reflection, we must, I think, conclude that such absolute freedom is an abstraction of the intellect, and that final determination to evil is inconsistent with what we believe of the omnipotence of love or the all-constraining power of goodness. 'That pure malignity can exist', Emerson has said,[2] 'is the extreme proposition of unbelief. It is not to be entertained by a rational agent; it is atheism, it is the last profanation.' Unless, therefore, *per impossibile*, a being were created wholly evil and impenetrable by good, he could not finally resist its influence. So long as any good at all remains in a nature, it is accessible to the spirit of God, and the little leaven must work till it leavens the whole lump.

But if we immerse ourselves thus in eschatological speculations as to what may happen after death to different people, we are in danger of forgetting that religious truth is in its essence practical, and addresses itself to the indi-

[1] As suggested in Burns's 'Address to the Deil'.

[2] In his essay on Swedenborg in *Representative Men*.

vidual soul. The truths of religion are to be taken neither as statements of future fact nor as a geography, so to speak, of the celestial regions. They are eternal truths of the spiritual life, which directly concern our spiritual bearing in the life that now is. This is as true of the belief in immortality as it is of any other religious truth. The idea of immortality has no religious significance, and it loses all credibility, if we separate it from the idea of eternal life as a realized possession. Apart from such a context, it becomes a sheer incongruity. 'There are people', it has been said, 'who cannot dispose of a day; an hour hangs heavy on their hands, and you offer them rolling ages without end.'[1] Hence in theories of ultimate restoration, it will be noted, the successive leases of life are not put forward as valuable in themselves, but only for the further opportunities they afford of laying hold on the life eternal. With that consummation the idea of the mere prolongation of existence in time seems to drop from us as no longer called for, as no longer adequate to the experience in question.

Not that we can discard the time-form altogether. Duration is an essential element in any notion we can form of reality; and we must clothe the thought of immortality in the language of time, if the meaning is not to evaporate altogether. If we try to avoid this necessity by speaking of an 'eternal now', a 'timeless present', we must convey into that 'now' the feeling of 'that which was and is and ever shall be': otherwise it shrinks to the abstraction of a mathematical point. The attempt to discard the durational form becomes in the end an affectation, which betrays us into a negative position actually falser (I have contended) than the popular crudities against which it is a protest. Nevertheless, as I have suggested, we do well

[1] Emerson.

to remember that the 'hope of immortality' is not to be regarded like the scientific prediction of an eclipse, or any other event in the temporal series. It is the supreme assertion of spiritual values, above all an assertion of the infinite value of the human spirit that has realized its vocation and entered into its heritage. And just for that reason the life beyond remains something which we cannot translate into concrete detail. In this region,

Alles Vergängliche ist nur ein Gleichniss.

'Beloved, *now* are we sons of God; and it doth not yet appear what we shall be.'

In the light of what has been said, we may ask, in conclusion, what ought our attitude to be towards death and an after-life. Two contrasted attitudes are obviously conceivable. Each has been widely exemplified in the history of mankind, and each can appeal to the authority of a great philosopher. Plato, in the *Phaedo*, as we saw, defined philosophy as a meditation of death, 'one long study of death and dying', seeing (he says) that 'only after we are dead can we gain the knowledge we desire'.[1] The true philosopher 'is in every respect at enmity with the body and longs to be released from the company of his enemy'. Till God releases him, his struggle is to 'live pure from the body, to have no communion or intercourse with it, beyond what is absolutely necessary'.[2] This mystic and ascetic strain, I pointed out, is very far from representing the whole of Plato's thought. Still the ascetic, other-worldly side is dominant in the *Phaedo*, and this was the aspect of his teaching which most impressed and attracted the Christian Fathers. The spirit of these sayings is the same spirit which, exaggerated in natures less sane and balanced, sent men to the desert as

[1] *Phaedo*, 62. [2] 66–8.

anchorites and pillar-saints, or drove them into monasteries that, by penance and asceticism becoming dead to this world, they might prepare for themselves an entrance into a heaven beyond. This is the temper of mind which has been labelled 'other-worldliness', and we deem it peculiarly characteristic of mediaeval Christian piety to regard the present life in this way as merely an antechamber to the never-ending life beyond. But the same contempt of the world, a still more complete subordination of the present to the future, is exhibited by any Indian fakir. It is refreshing to recall, by way of contrast, the old Persian consecration of the wholesome activities of life. 'He who sows corn sows holiness.' 'To do so is more meritorious than a hundred acts of adoration, a thousand oblations, ten thousand sacrifices.'[1] In such extreme forms as I have mentioned, this exclusive preoccupation with future salvation would be generally condemned by modern sentiment. But even when it does not run into such excesses—even when it flowers in natures of a delicate and tender beauty—the negative attitude adopted to the present life and its concerns is indefensible: the dualism between the present and the future is wrong in principle.

Let us hear the other philosopher. '*Homo liber de nulla re minus quam de morte cogitat*', says Spinoza;[2] 'there is nothing on which the free man lets his thoughts dwell less than on death.' '*Et ejus sapientia,*' he adds, with an obvious allusion to Plato, '*non mortis sed vitae meditatio est*'; 'the free man's wisdom is not a meditation of death but of life.' In the same spirit Goethe would have us substitute for the old maxim, '*memento mori*', the truer motto, *Gedenke zu leben, memento vivere,* remember to live. And in our own generation there is Lewis Nettleship's often quoted saying, in one of his last letters, 'Don't bother about death; it doesn't count.' It was the spirit of his own life

[1] Cf. Stevenson's 'Our Lady of the Snows'. [2] *Ethics*, IV. 67.

as expressed in the beautiful inscription on the memorial tablet in Balliol Chapel: 'He loved great things and thought little of himself: desiring neither fame nor influence, he won the devotion of men and was a power in their lives: and seeking no disciples, he taught to many the greatness of the world and of man's mind.'

The meaning of Nettleship's advice is that physical death cannot touch the life of the spirit. If we are occupied with 'thoughts immortal and divine', or with some great cause which means for us the kingdom of God upon earth, or, for the matter of that, in doing anything that we feel is worth doing, we have neither time nor inclination to brood over our personal future. Our life is full of these objective interests. So death should find us; and to a mind so attuned physical death ought to appear no more than an incident in life, an event to be accepted as naturally as sleep. It should bring with it no depressing suggestion of finality, nor do we find that it really does so in those who thus live. 'Unbelief in death', it has been said, 'seems to be the necessary characteristic or concomitant of true spiritual life.'[1] And spiritual life in this connexion is not to be limited to religious experience in any narrow or traditional sense of the word. It means the super-individual life in any form. Such is the life we ought to live to our life's end. Other preparation for death there can in any case be none. The very idea of specific preparation for death and a future life (as if the new life were to be entirely different in kind from the old, with no continuity between the two) can have no meaning for those who have sought and found eternal life here—

> in the very world, which is the world
> Of all of us,—the place where in the end
> We find our happiness, or not at all.[2]

[1] Edward Caird, *Evolution of Religion*, ii. 242 (3rd edition).

[2] Wordsworth, *The Prelude*, Bk. XI. The passage in which the lines occur was published separately at an earlier date.

INDEX

Absorption, two senses of, 161-2.
'Active Reason', 43, 66-8, 152.
Adam, James, 26.
Alger, W. R., 121-2.
Animism, 7, 74.
Aristotle, 40-1, 43, 51, 62-71, 152-5.
Arnold, Matthew, 172, 189, 192, 196.
Aurelius, Marcus, 163, 187-8.
Averroes, 67-8.
Avicenna, 67.

Bacon, Francis, 200.
Bosanquet, B., 152-9, 189.
Bowne, B. P., 101 n.
Bradley, A. C., 121 n.
Bradley, F. H., 85, 125, 128, 156-9, 178.
Browning, 199, 202-3.
Buddhism, 110, 113-14, 116-17, 130, 139.
Burnet, Prof. J., 21, 33.
Burns, 204.
Butler, Bishop, 168, 171-2, 175.

Caird, Edward, 195 n., 208.
Carlyle, 180.
Cave, Sidney, 108, 110.
Charles, Archdeacon, 15-16, 182 n.
Clifford, W. K., 85, 181.
Coleridge, 88.
Comte, 90.
Consensus gentium, argument from, 2-4.
Continuance, theories of, 13.

Dante, 133, 160-1, 190, 197.
Davids, Prof. Rhys, 110, 112-13.
Davids, Mrs. Rhys, 111, 113, 117, 146.
Descartes, 83, 88.
Deussen, P., 115-16.
Dill, Samuel, 188.
Dionysus, cult of, 23-5.
Dougall, Miss L., 122, 129.

Edwards, Jonathan, 174.
Eliot, George, 164.
Emerson, 193 n., 204-5.
Empedocles, 107.
Epictetus, 184-5, 187.
Epiphenomenalism, 84-6.
Euripides, 23.

Fall of the soul, in Orphism, 26; in Plato, 36.
Farnell, L. R., 22-3, 25, 32.
Frazer, Sir J. G., 4-6, 10-11.
Fowler, W. Warde, 17 n.

Galloway, Principal George, 185 n.
Goethe, 22, 139, 196-8, 206-7.
Green, T. H., 95.

Hades, 19-21.
Harrison, Miss J., 25 n., 27 n.
Hawthorne, Nathaniel, 195.
Hegel, 51, 146.
Heine, 131-2.
Henley, W. E., 186.
Hogg, Prof. A. G., 110, 115 n.
Holmes, Edmond, 120-1.
Horace, 183.
Hügel, Baron F. von, 19 n.
Hume, criticism of the identical self, 96-9; on immortality, 198-9.
Huxley, T. H., 84, 112.

Ibsen, 201-2.
Inge, Dean, 190 n.

James, William, 79, 85, 87, 97-8, 100.
Jones, Sir Henry, 193 n., 202 n.
Joyce, G. C., 132.
Jowett, Benjamin, 35, 50.

Kant, 56, 75 n., 95-6, 118, 134, 153-4, 169, 175-9.
Karma, 108-22, 154, 173, 180.
Keats, 137, 139.
Kipling, 46.

Labadie, 161-2.
Laird, Prof. J., 78 n., 104.
Leibniz, 81 n., 83, 89, 125.
Lessing, 4.
Lightfoot, Bishop, 186.

Locke, 2, 74–6, 201.
Lotze, 77–82, 93–5.
Lucretius, 174.
Luther, 181–2.

Macdonald, George, 193.
McDougall, W., 74, 82, 94, 102–3, 180, 182.
Mackintosh, Prof. H. R., 140 n., 166 n.
McTaggart, J. M. E., 123–7, 168.
Maeterlinck, 12.
Maher, M., 69, 92.
Massillon, 181.
Materialism, 83–4.
Mellone, S. H., 133 n.
Mill, J. S., 170–1.
Milton, 131, 182.
Mysticism, 161–2.
Myth in Plato, function of, 51–3.

Nettleship, Lewis, 207–8.
Nicholas of Cusa, 190 n.
Nirvana, 145–6.

Organism, a natural unity, 89; an analogue of the self-conscious life, 93.
Orphism, 25–32; in Plato, 60.

Parallelism, psycho-physical, 86–7.
Parmenides, 38.
Paul, St., 27, 59, 115, 142–3, 155, 181.
Paulsen, F., 103.
Pre-existence of soul, in Orphism, 26; in Plato, 35.
Pindar, 24, 28–9.
Plato, 26, 28–9, 30–1, Lecture III *passim*, 62, 64, 104, 108–9, 117, 119, 127, 152, 164, 170, 173, 182, 196, 206–7.
Plutarch, 31, 131.
Psyche, in Homer, 21; in Plato, 33 ff.
Pythagoras, 33 n., 46, 107.

Reabsorption, 162–7.
Reid, Thomas, 93–4.
Renan, 182.
Rewards and Punishments, 14, 53–4, 118–20, 172–81.
Robertson, F. W., 117.
Rohde, E., 24, 27.
Royce, Josiah, 192.
Russell, Bertrand, 136, 194.

Salmond, S. D. F., 12 n., 144.
Schiller, 139.
Schiller, F. C. S., 131 n.
Schleiermacher, 135–6, 164.
Schopenhauer, 138–9, 167.
Seneca, 186–8.
Shakespeare, 8, 107, 109, 131.
Sheol, 15.
Sidgwick, Henry, 175–9, 183.
Smith, Sir George A., 185.
Socrates, 34, 38, 47, 57, 104.
Sollas, W. J., 1 n.
Spencer, Herbert, 12 n.
Spenser, 132.
Spinoza, 53–4, 83, 136–7, 148–52, 155, 182, 207.
Stevenson, R. L., 185, 207.
Stewart, Prof. J. A., 56.
Stirling, J. H., 184.
Stoics, 163, 185–90.
Stout, Prof. G. F., 84, 86–7, 101.
Substantiality of the soul, 72 ff., 123–4.
Swinburne, 132.

Taylor, Prof. A. E., 183–5.
Tennyson, 102, 130, 165–6, 184.
Troeltsch, E., 166–7.
Tucker, Abraham, 129.
Tylor, E. B., 7, 9, 12–13, 106, 110–11.

Unity or simplicity of soul, argument from, 73.
Unity of consciousness, in Lotze, 94; in Kant, 95–6.

Vaughan, Henry, 47.
Vitalism, Lotze's campaign against, 81; neo-vitalism, 90–1.
Vogt, Carl, 83.

Ward, Prof. James, 71, 85, 87, 89, 198.
Webb, Prof. C. C. J., 51 n.
Wordsworth, 2, 161, 198, 208.

Xenophanes, 107.

Printed in England at the Oxford University Press